I AM
ALIVE IN
LOS ANGELES!

I AM
ALIVE IN
LOS ANGELES!

by
Mike the PoeT

iUniverse, Inc.
New York Lincoln Shanghai

I am Alive In Los Angeles!

iUniverse books may be ordered through booksellers or by contacting:

iUniverse
2021 Pine Lake Road, Suite 100
Lincoln, NE 68512
www.iuniverse.com
1-800-Authors (1-800-288-4677)

COVER & DESIGN BY MEAR ONE www.mearone.com

DRAWINGS ON CHAPTER 3 & 6 BY EMI M. CANNIBAL FLOWER/THINKSPACE

ISBN-13: 978-0-595-39520-0 (pbk)
ISBN-13: 978-0-595-83919-3 (ebk)
ISBN-10: 0-595-39520-1 (pbk)
ISBN-10: 0-595-83919-3 (ebk)

Printed in the United States of America

BLESSED BE THE PEACEMAKERS!
TEACH LOVE
& WORK WITH URGENCY!!
Mikethepoet@comcast.net
www.ksdmusic.com
www.poetix.net
www.getunderground.com

CONTENTS

Note to Readers.

To signify is to breathe something in, To breathe something out—to give it a life all its own.

Mike is a signifier. Mike signifies Los Angeles with a highly developed native sensibility that reveals subtleties, shades, and tones well past the obvious. Time and place becomes the know of a place on an intimate human scale:

—Los Angeles and all its ramifications and vibrations and well beyond through the eyes, the heart, the brain of MIke the Poet.

He breathes hope in language that shimmers depicting what we often times fail to see but what we most definitely feel. His love affair becomes our love affair; we become a part of the journey our selves and all hail Los Angeles.

Phillip Martin.

"Before you earn the right to rap any sort of joint,
you have to love it a little while."

Nelson Algren

Chicago: City on the Make

I am a 3rd generation LA native. Both of my parents were born in Los Angeles. The stories of my grandparents started this. My grandmother spent her childhood hiking the hills of Highland Park, Eagle Rock & Mt. Washington. Her tales of sheepherders on the green slopes of Highland Park are hard to believe. Her father was a homesteader & built their home off York Blvd & Ave 60 just before my grandmother was born in 1917.

My mom's father Frank Sibley told me about riding the streetcars from his house @ 42nd & Avalon to the massive theaters a few miles north in the broadway entertainment district. His stories about the great depression, long roads, orange groves & the Second World War were epic.

"Ready! Begin."

His parents met in Mexico City in 1911. My great grandfather John Sibley worked for the Union Pacific railroad as an interpreter. He met my great-grandmother Julia Rivera in Mexico City. In March 1918 after Pancho Villa took the Rivera family's land, my great-grandparents and her 7 sisters moved to Los Angeles just in time for the birth of Grandpa Frank @ Queen of Angels hospital.

My parents went to Washington High School in Los Angeles off 108th & Normandie. They met their senior year with a group of friends at the Rose Parade. In 1966 they married after both graduating from Long Beach State. I was born on St. Patrick's day in 1974 at St. Mary's Hospital in Long Beach. My parents split in 1976.

I grew up in Cerritos attending Artesia High School in Lakewood. By age 7 I had a collection of maps & knew the freeway system. I loved geography from day one. The friends I grew up with in Cerritos were truly a diverse lot. We were the United Nations. We grew up going to the mall, playing basketball & watching the Lakers. We were a motley crew of Korean, Ecudorean, African-American, Mexican & Filipino kids. I was damn near the only the white boy. We knew we were a part of a new breed. Ironically we were the class of 1992, the year Rodney King asked, "Can't we all just get along?"

I started at UCLA in the Fall of 1992. This is when my pen became my best friend & poetry really began. Early days at UCLA were lengthy LA drive missions to every pocket of the metropolis, journal in hand. The first prose poems came from majestic rides with Henry & Phil. Graduating in 1997, my favorite courses were in Urban Planning.
Right away, I applied for Graduate School with UCLA's incredible Urban Planning Department but they rejected me & told me to get some real world work experience. They did me a great favor, because ever since then I've been an underground urban planner.

I make the city my museum like the Chicago School of Architecture used to say. Shortly after I graduated, I got my commercial driver's license & began tourguiding up & down the West Coast. I drove a 15-passenger van from L.A. to the Sierra Nevada's, Vegas, Grand Canyon & San Francisco. The magical characters I met along the way inspired hundreds of poems. When I wasn't on the road, I was home with PhiLLharmoniC woodshedding. We planted the seeds for the Poets of the RoundTable back in 97-98 with poetry sessions like Underwords & the House of Green.

After living in the same house for the first 18 years, I've had 11 apartments in the city of Los Angeles since 1992. Westwood, West LA, Culver City, Hollywood, Country Club Park, Koreatown. One of my favorites was called the Shangri Lodge. The roaches that were there were there long before me.

Being alive in Los Angeles means driving. It means having friends in a hundred neighborhoods. Everyday I figure 8 my way thru the blood & bones of the city. I love geography—these journeys invigorate me.
Connecting the dots is what I like to do from the hilltop parties to the Watts Towers, North Long Beach to Frogtown, there's so much flavor—landscapes & characters. I love it all.

Over the years i've zig-zagged the LA region with meticulous precision & to this day I still find new pockets. Los Angeles is a puzzle to me that I have spent my life putting together. Somewhere along the journey I started writing it all down so I could remember.

Being alive in Los Angeles means heat waves in December and countless afternoons eating some incredibly spicy food. Lovin' every minute of it.

The real Los Angeles is enjoying home-cooked meals in backyard bungalows from Glassell Park to Cudahy, Huntington Beach to Inglewood.Carne asada, sushi, falafel, pho. 213, 323, 310, 562, 714, 626. I soak it up like a sponge. Here it is. I love L.A!
I am alive in LOS Angeles!!

1 ROCKIN THE POPULACE

I am alive in Los Angeles!

I am alive in Los Angeles!
Here in the wild, wild west.
The warm wind hits my face,

I walk across stained concrete,

I cry tears of joy on Flower Street.

I watch families dancing

on their porches on Christmas Eve.

I smile widely.

I move thru the city,

my heart beating swiftly

as sirens speed by me.

I revel in the sadness—my soul is deep

I take full responsibility.
Give me everything!
It hurts—it's so beautiful!
The universal
soulful
multicultural
Emerging
worldwide
tribe people!

I am alive in Los Angeles!
I am alive in Los Angeles!
Where the angles change like isosceles. Citywide topographies
undulate across massive landscape
moving from chain-link to palatial gates into separate economic
states with rising birth rates below hilltops in the streetscapes.
One can barely even equivocate The fluctuations in rent
so evident all across from
block to block to block…

Extravagance and adversity interlock:
palatial spots, crosswalks, burrito shops,
housekeepers hanging out at bus stops,
the Country Club's all walled off.
The city's blowing up like a molotov
even when I'm in the shower
I hear the horns honk.
I am alive in Los Angeles!
Driving listening to Miles Davis
Or electronic music
I move thru traffic
Loving the inner-city dynamics
the midcity magic moves from happiness to tragic,
adversity to extravagance.
Seeing Korean grandparents moving slowly
& Catholic school children crossing fearlessly
I saw a stray dog that looked like Spud Mackenzie
Wandering by the *Belmont Tunnel* on 2nd Street
live and direct in the Rampart District.
I am alive in Los Angeles!

On warm winter days when
the Santa Ana winds blow
L.A. folks get a little more irritable.
Tight traffic makes folks real close
below brown clouds of smoke.
Buses blow by packed wall to wall,
dogs howl & the warm winds blow.

I AM ALIVE IN Los Angeles!

LA MYTHS

LOS ANGELES IS THE EPICENTER OF MYTH MAK-
ING. IMAGES OF LOS ANGELES RUN THE GAMUT.
HOLLYWOOD USES ALL OF THESE EXTREMES.
POPULAR CULTURE ADDRESSES LOS ANGELES
COMIC INCONGRUITIES. THE ONLY IMAGE NOT PRO-
JECTED IS THE MUNDANE.
LA IS BOTH A MICROCOSM AND MACROCOSM OF
PHENOMENA LIKE:

SUNSHINE	NOIR
GLAMOUR	SALSA
BAYWATCH	BLADE RUNNER
EARTHQUAKE	APOCALYPSE
CATASTROPHE	RAMONA
UTOPIA	HELL
BEACH BOYS	NWA
EL NINO	OCEAN BREAZES
HOOKERS	MODELS
PALM TREES	FREEWAYS
PRODUCERS	HOMELESS
SURFERS	CHOLOS
ANGELYNE	MADONNA
UNDERGROUND	HOLLYWOOD

Pockets.

Within the 468 square miles of Los Angeles city limits there are hundreds of neighborhoods.

Over the last few years blue signs have begun appearing in local neighborhoods designating their specific district within LA city limits.

Cheviot Hills Mar Vista St. Andrews Square Elysian Valley Lincoln Heights Montecito Heights Garvanza Glassell Park Highland Park Cypress Park Canterbury Knolls Morningside Circle Hermon Athens on A Hill Chesterfield Square Wellington Square Arlington Heights Harvard Heights Studio City Whitley Heights West Adams Country Club Park Angeles Mesa Mt. Washington Eagle Rock Leimert Park Valley Village Encino Sherman Oaks Chinatown Echo Park El Sereno Crown Hill Gallery Row Koreatown Rampart Historic Filipinotown Silverlake Century City Westwood King Estates Brentwood Palms Pico-Robertson Carthay Circle Jefferson Park Manchester Square Toluca Lake Temple-Beaudry Angelino Heights Miracle Mile Hyde Park Hollywood!
This still isn't all of 'em.

LA AUTHORS

Is it the sunshine or catastrophes,
flash floods or the traffic?

Something about Los Angeles
makes music, makes magic.
The muse of Los Angeles
Makes artists get active.
Behold the lore of LA authors!

Who's rockin' the populace
In the postmodern metropolis?

LA AuthorS…
Starting with Charles Fletcher Lummis Sunshine looms large In literary Los Angeles. From the myth of *Ramona* & California ranchos, Orange groves & the *Arroyo Seco*—Expatriate artists of the 1890s the first sunshine wave of LA Authors.Boosters blew the trumpets On the golden state's landscape, sun for 300 days, a cure for old age, Find the fountain of youth in Los Angeles. Hyped up pamphlets
Let the world know. "Land of the sunshine," "the new Eden." It was manifest destiny, but not heaven for everybody. Besides the boosters there were debunkers, socialists, expatriate poets, leftist screenwriters.Fitzgerald, Robinson Jeffers, *Louis Adamic*, Jake Zeitlin, Nathaniel West was one of the best, the city in flames in the *Day of the Locust*. The underground intelligentsia of artists & authors living in Echo Park bungalows, McCarthy called it red hill.
Sinclair yelled *Oil!*
   Behold! The lore of LA Authors!

Chandler & Cain were kings of writing noir
detective novels in the lost streets
of Bunker Hill where Fante celebrates
staircase fire escapes & lost love.
Long before Rodney King
there was the Zoot Suit Riots, the LAPD
& Navy fools fought with Pachucos in the Sleepy Lagoon Carey
McWilliams knew the deal
on the Fire *Factories in the Field*
Palm trees are swaying in the wind
As the sunset begins it's twilight on Franklin.
What makes Sammy run? Is it the architectural illusion?
Hollywood tycoons & the American dream
If He Hollers Let Him Go, Central Avenue
Robinson Jeffers & Langston Hughes
Ray Bradbury wrote about *Martian Chronicles,*
L. Ron Hubbard wrote science fiction into scientology,
Bukowski in single room occupancies wrote sublime poetry About
the plight of modern man with a beer can in his hands. Venice beats
off Abbott Kinney
Every time I'm in Venice
Jim Morrison speaks to me! Behold the lore of LA authors!
Rockin' like Rockabilly car clubs, the Carpenters, Beach Boys. Grease,
disco & roller skating
Singer-songwriters in Laurel Canyon
like Neil Young, James Taylor & Joni Mitchell sang the real deal in the
Hollywood hills basking above Babylon & hedonism
before hippie folk maidens became pop rock musicians. Rockin' the
Rainbow Room & Led Zeppelin
sellin platinum radio free Hollywood
Hotel California Doobie Brothers
Play that funky music white boy.
Behold! The lore of LA Authors!

Brett Easton Ellis tells us about
Gilded youth snorting white rails
In Beverly Hills, *Less than Zero*
Walter Mosley with Easy Rawlins
The Devil in the Blue Dress & Little Richard
Barry White grew up near Willowbrook
Motown came out west with the Jacksons
Lewis MacAdams dug Miles
he wrote *the Birth of the Cool*
James Ellroy kept *LA Confidential* like *Black Dahlia*
To Gabriel Garcia Marquez Magical realism.
Hunter S. Thompson's New journalism
Carolyn See Jervey Tervalon
Jerry Stahl @ Skylight Books.
We're South of no north
in the *City of Quartz,*
Reelin' in the years in the *Ecology of Fear*
Mike Davis & *Magical Urbanism* hit like
Joan Didion's *White Album*
Thomas Pynchon to Luis Rodriguez,
Lynell George to Ruben Martinez
Wanda Coleman & Exene Cervenka.
KROQ to KDAY sound selectors.
Punk rock pop Underground poets.
Urban planners, Klein, Soja, Jello Biafra,
Rollins Ellyn Maybe spoken word artists
Got trails blazin' Paul Vangelisti,
John Thomas, Lawrence Lipton
& *the Holy Barbarians,*
Stuart Perkoff & words raisin' roofs like
A Mic & Dim Lights Poetix *Beyond Baroque.*
Ginsberg got naked folks.
Welcome to the West Coast's Poetry & Jazz Festival
Behold the lore of LA authors!

The truth is
stranger than Fiction
its surreal living these conditions,
William Gibson Science Fiction.
Cyber punks on super expressways.
Ghetto bird cameras everyday.
Hollywood loves the apocalypse
The coast is toast!
Earthquakes flash floods El Nino
Armageddon busted bridges
Waves are crashing on the edge of the continent.
The city in flames or another day in paradise
Sunshine or noir—
Baywatch or *Blade Runner*?
Stay tuned for another long hot summer
Santa Ana warm winds keep blowin'
& creative juices keep flowin',
the list of LA authors keeps growin'
LA Authors makin' Music loud like
Sunset Strip rock'n'roll soul
Doors Van Halen Motley Crue Guns'n'Roses
Ice Cube, NWA Dr. Dre, Pharcyde
Snoop Dogg, Freestyle Fellowship,
Hip-hop, metal, bedroom producers,
Turntablists & poets

Behold the lore of LA Authors!

11 GREAT BOOKS ABOUT L.A.

CITY OF QUARTZ
by Mike Davis

SOUTHLAND
by Nina Revoyr

IF HE HOLLERS LET HIM GO
by Chester Himes

HISTORY OF FORGETTING
by Norman Klein

AN ISLAND ON THE LAND
by Carey McWilliams

HOLLYWOOD
by Charles Bukowski

DREAMS FROM BUNKER HILL
by John Fante

ALWAYS RUNNING
by Luis Rodriguez

THE RIVER
by Lewis MacAdams

MY DARK PLACES
by James Ellroy

THE RIOT INSIDE ME
by Wanda Coleman

11 GREAT LA ALBUMS

Chavez Ravine—RY COODER

The Edge—David Axelrod

Straight Outta Compton—NWA

Leimert Park—KAAMAU DAAOOD

The World is a Ghetto—WAR

Guero—BECK

Rapping Black in a White World—WATTS PROPHETS

Battle for Los Angeles—RAGE AGAINST THE MACHINE

Los Angeles—X

Lady in the Canyon—Joni Mitchell

Nothing's Shocking—JANE'S ADDICTION

ANYTHING BY
RED HOT CHILI PEPPERS
The DOORS

EMAIL ME YOURS…

2 Marshlands &
willow thickets...

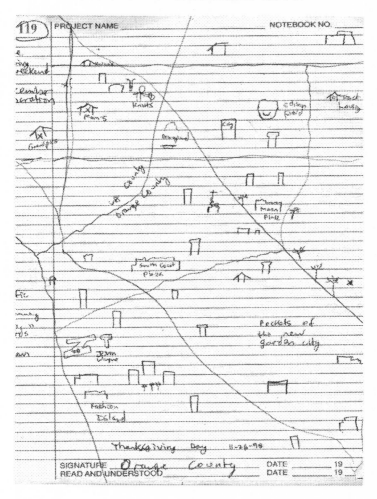

Here's a poem
about Long Beach.

THE 562

The 562 is a nexus:
A suburban, urban cross-section.
A small town big city,
affluent, yet gritty,
The 562 is somewhere between
Hollywood & Irvine,
Santa Monica & Anaheim.
The 562 is a good time 'cuz
its people are down to Earth.
Blessed by birth to be born
Where the vibes are warm,
Catch that cool ocean breeze
Blowing in from the beach.
The clouds come from the south
As the coast winds
around the peninsula
of Palos Verdes.
The temperature is perfect.
This land was once
marshlands
& Willow thickets,
Intercepted by the L.A River,
Now surfers & grandparents kick it.
The 562 is all-American multicultural,
Folks from Iowa to Cambodia,
El Salvador to Ethiopia,
Aviation Okies &
The aerospace industry.

Denizens OF Long Beach
Groove to Snoop Dogg & Sublime,
Garage rock & Freestyle rhyme.
On the streets of Long Beach
you can find
oil in Signal Hill,
Broadway's
alternative lifestyles-
Art in the East Village, Downtown lofts &
Rockabilly chillers!
How many Poly players are in the NFL?!
From Joe Jost's to the Prospector, Cohiba,
Blue Nile to The Blue Cafe,
Drinking Sangria on a hot day,
Barflies cruise from the 49er to Belmont Shore,
Fern's to the V-Room.
The 562 is a window into the future
with lots of history.
Like the powerful earthquake of '33,
The Pike is the place to be,
We salute Cameron Diaz
& her flavorful family.
Respect to Lakewood, Cerritos, Bellflower, Paramount,
Hawaiian Gardens, Whittier, Norwalk,
Cudahy,South Gate, Compton
to damn near Bell Gardens.
Not to be confused with the 310, This is The *562*!
In the middle of So. Cal, but its own little world,
It's another beautiful day at El Dorado Park,
in the place
of my birth
& the home of my heart...

Window into a LosT Long BeacH

Millions of years ago Long Beach was underwater and Signal Hill was an island. Small foothills like Signal Hill, the Baldwin Hills, Palos Verdes and the Cheviot Hills peaked up from the Pacific Ocean. These hills rose up from the Newport-Inglewood Fault, the same fault responsible for the 1933 earthquake in Long Beach.

As time went on the San Gabriel Mountain Range evolved, creating the flood plain that is the Los Angeles basin. The great height of these mountains coupled with the proximity to the ocean makes the Southland the most flood-prone ecology of any major urban city in America.

Long Beach is situated between the San Gabriel River and the Los Angeles River. Most residents are familiar with the path of these two waterways; but they know them as the 605 and 710 Freeways. Perhaps only Long Beach residents well into their 70s even understand how influential these two rivers have been in the development of the LBC.

Though in their present form they are small streams in polluted concrete channels; both of these rivers after heavy rain have recorded rushing volumes of water comparable to grand waterways like the Colorado and Mississippi.

The Los Angeles and San Gabriel River watershed is an incredible ecosystem. In its natural state grizzly bears once roamed the banks of its waters. The land that is now Long Beach was marshlands and willow thickets. Much of the Southern California basin from Glendale, Eagle Rock, Beverly Hills, West Los Angeles, Torrance, Compton—all of this land held pockets of swamps and dense, wooded vegetation.

Furthermore, these rivers also have several smaller tribu
taries like the Rio Hondo, Arroyo Seco, Compton Creek,
Verdugo Wash and Los Coyotes Creek. Local writer and
Lakewood City official DJ Waldie in his book *Holy Land*,
says that before these rivers were paved, locals called them
"tramp rivers" because every year they found a new bed.
Most of all these rivers were unpredictable. The San Ga
briel River once emptied into the ocean where the LA River
does now. In 1867 a great flood changed the San Gabriel's
course.
The LA River once emptied into the ocean via the Ballona Creek
near Venice and Marina Del Rey. Its course changed southward to
Long Beach in 1825. The force of the 1825 flood was so powerful that
it cut a new waterway south.
Now the LA River empties into the ocean between Long Beach and
San Pedro.
The San Gabriel River meets the ocean where Seal Beach
meets Long Beach. The Gabrielino Indians had many vil
lages along the waters of these rivers. One of them was
located on the present location of Cal State Long Beach.
The rivers provided all they needed to survive. Within the
ecology of the rivers were an ample variety of edible plants
and animals.
The Gabrielino relied on the rivers and marshes for almost every
facet of their existence. They even made their huts with poles from
the willow thickets. The Gabrielino remained undisturbed well into
the 18th Century. Not until the Spanish occupation of California did
this change. In
1784 the land of present day Long Beach was deeded to a retiring
Spanish soldier Manuel Nieto. A land grant of
approximately 200,000 acres that included all the land
from the Los Angeles River to the Santa Ana River. Nieto's descen-
dants sold the land to the Bixby family.

Eventually one of the Bixby brothers leased some of the
land to a man named William Willmore. Willmore was
Long Beach's first developer. For awhile Long Beach was
called *Willmore City*. In 1884 the name changed to Long
Beach.

As the 20th Century began so did the real estate boom.

Long Beach developers were ill-prepared for the flood menace. Being
situated between the two rivers made Long Beach perhaps the most
vulnerable area in all of Southern California. In 1938, 87 people in LA
County died in the floods caused by El Nino. Residents were forced to
use boats to get supplies. Bridges were washed away and houses
floated from their foundations.

Equally powerful floods occurred in 1889, 1914 and 1934.

Besides human casualties, these floods wiped out millions
of dollars of real estate. When the rains came Lakewood
was literally a lake. Maps from the 1938 Flood show the
most heavily flooded areas of the 1938 calamity were in
what is now Cerritos, Hawaiian Gardens, east Long Beach
and low-lying areas around Compton and Inglewood.

It's no coincidence that the most flood-prone areas often
became ghettos.

The area of North Long Beach would often be under five feet of water
when the rains came. Watts was known as Mudtown. Paramount was
once called Clearwater. The same is true in areas of West Long Beach and
Hawaiian Gardens.

Hawaiian Gardens during the Depression was originally populated
by Okies and Mexicans who worked in the dairy farms of Cypress
and Cerritos, then known as Dairy Valley. The Los Coyotes Creek
and San Gabriel River intersect in Hawaiian Gardens, adjacent to El
Dorado Park.

Shortly after the floods of 1938 the United States Army Corps of Engineers began working earnestly towards paving the beds of both rivers. Hundreds of millions of dollars and hundreds of tons of concrete were poured into the project. Trees and vegetation were removed from the banks and concrete replaced the sandy bottom.

By the mid-1950s there was little trace of the river's natural state. What remains is hundreds of miles of dams, concrete channels and bridges. These days both rivers often seem more like sewers. Trash floats in their waters and homeless bathe below the bridges.

It is this tragic state that has led to groups like The Friends of the Los Angeles River (FoLAR). Every spring since 1989, FoLAR has produced *La Gran Limpieza*, the Great Los Angeles River Clean-Up. On average they remove over 30 tons of garbage from the River each year. What began with a dozen people at one site the first year has grown to an effort involving two thousand people at ten sites along the river's length.

FoLAr was started by Lewis MacAdams as a 40-year-performance-art piece in 1986.

Initially it was just him and a few of his friends. Now Fo LAR boasts several thousand members. The movement be gan by FoLAR has also helped spearhead efforts to restore the San Gabriel River and the wetlands in Long Beach.

The City of Long Beach is embarking on a plan to bring more open space to the city. They see the wetlands as a vi able retreat from the ever-increasing urbanization. Restora tion sites in Long Beach include five along the L.A. River, the Colorado Lagoon, and three areas in East Long Beach near El Dorado Park.

Recently the Colorado Lagoon was awarded a $200,000 grant by the California Coastal Conservancy. In addition to pending proposals, other grants have also been awarded at the Sixth Street Wetland.

Long Beach's natural ecology is being nursed back to health. Groups like FoLaR, Friends of the San Gabriel River, Friends of the Colorado Lagoon and the Long Beach RiverLink are working diligently one victory at a time.

On a balmy April afternoon, I drove to where the Los Angeles River crosses Willow Street. Here the concrete channel gives way to the soft rock bottom as the river meets the Pacific Ocean a few miles south. I observe a lone fish swimming on the centimeter-high water running on the concrete bed. Most of his body is above water, it can hardly be called swimming. Yet he flips around doing aquatic cartwheels. We watch him enter the slightly deeper water at the threshold where concrete breaks into soft-rock bottom.

It is here south of Willow Street where we could see a window into how the River once flowed in Long Beach. Rare birds still live in this ecology. Though shipyards and oil wells dot the surrounding landscape, nature still holds court.

Like the single lone fish we saw swimming, it is this glimmer of hope that keeps men like Lewis MacAdams working to save the river.

I asked MacAdams what he and FoLAR hoped for in regards to Long Beach and the Los Angeles River. "Our goal is to create a 52-mile long emerald bracelet, a Los Angeles River Greenway from the mountains to the sea, and I always look on Long Beach as the PROOF—of Riverwatch, the year-round water quality monitoring program that we're about to begin—our Los Angeles River Clean-up that takes 30 tons or so of garbage out of the river that would otherwise end up on Long Beach's beaches; of our alternative approaches to flood protection that we're battling for that protect the vast flood plain of the Los Angeles and San Gabriel Rivers (including most of Long Beach from floods without pouring more concrete.)"

"If the river through Long Beach is healthy, then the rest of the river is healthy, too. One of these days the southernmost steel head run will return to the Los Angeles River, and as the trout start their journey upstream they'll nod to their left to the Queen Mary (the toothpick in the mouth of the river) and to their right to the Long Beach citizens recreating in Cesar Chavez Park and set their sights north towards the San Gabriels, and as they pass beneath the Sunnynook Footbridge in Atwater I or my ghost and I will be leaning over the railing waving as they swim by."

WHERE HAVE ALL THE ORANGE GROVES GONE?

Imagine miles & miles
of orange groves,
rows & rows of fragrant citrus fields
& just a few roads,
this was once the landscape
of the Golden State.
Orange groves!

WHERE HAVE ALL THE ORANGE GROVES GONE?
EVERYWHERE the corporate shopping mall theme per
meates.
It's the exploitation of space across the city marketplace. Multi-
national corporate gates are the new evolving
cityscape.
Simulated theme space has made the global rat race
the most familiar place wherever you grace your face.
The international franchise nest has met the multiplex.
Consumer business complexes are proliferating across the
continent. Next to freeways of traffic apocalypse.
This is the new suburban metropolis.
The economic octopus has swallowed up mom and pops.
it's lavish landscapes dense in Mcdonaldized reference.
The themed presence is pervasive while history is being erased.
The drive for developing profit
forgot to consider the cost
of destroying our lost landscape,
The dollar stakes chase has replaced
former meanings of community and space. Now we got consumer
culture & the rat race.

Where have all the Orange groves gone?

Two Twilight Drives

The year was 1985,

Sky-high flames were fueling a fire blaze at dusk. We were driving by on the 405 in summer twilight seeing towering flames smoking above the steel beams and septic tanks of the refinery.

The oil refinery was burning over in Carson. The freeway was crowded just after sunset, the twilight shadows sat orange as fire clouds rose high over hundreds of cars. Time froze with the image.

You needed sunglasses after the sun left. An inferno of surreal brightness. We were going to Kaiser to see my grandfather. I was riding with my sister, mom and grandmother while the sky burned. My eyes burned like my mind imprinted the vibrant vision. Time suspended like the world was ending

I can still see it.

Another twilight evening a few years before around 1982 my mom and I were driving. We were on the 605 freeway heading to my grandparent's house in Long Beach. We hadn't even been on the freeway for one exit when out of the blue we saw a man standing on the side of the road. He looked a lot like *Fernando Valenzuela*.

This was in the early 1980's right around Fernandomania.

I can still see the brave man's face.
We were in the far right lane. Just as we were about to pass him, he jumped right in front of our car.
Thump! We smacked him.
He flew several feet in the air. He flew up on top of the hood flopping like a Raggedy Ann doll. Through the windshield I watched him flying.
Mom had put on the brakes but it was too late.
Our light blue Ford Malibu hit the Fernando look-alike. He ran right in front of our car with no fear. Dancing with the devil for thrills, my man was resilient.
When the ambulance and cops came he got up by himself.

He walked right into the ambulance.

Later we found out he was on PCP.

He tried to commit suicide but all he got was a free ride.

I'll never forget his face.

1992

In 1992
I graduated
from high school
In 1992 L.A. hosted
the Rodney King uprisings.
In 1992 the LAPD crowned
Rodney King.
In 1992
I lost my virginity.
I started at U.C.L.A.
in 1992.
Back in 1992
I started my education,
epic city missions east to west.
PHaRCyDE & A Tribe Called QuesT.

1992 is when it all started.

3 THE REAL HOLLYWOOD

HOLLYWOOD

Hooray for Hollywood!

That's ENTERTAINMENT!

There's Hollywood the industry
and Hollywood the neighborhood.
One word conjures up endless implications
And the furthest reaches of your imagination.
Ranging from sleazy city blocks
to Fortune 500 corporations,
titillating images and the lost generation.
One hit wonders & B-Movie actors
personal assistants & executive mistresses.
Stunt men & Kung-fu fighters.
Fly-by-nighters & vampires.
Liar! Liar! You won't find
your church choir in Hollywood.
On late nights you might see
a Mr. T look-alike at Popeye's chicken.
Rock & roll gypsies kick it at the Whisky.
Hollywood's underbelly is populated
by Two-bit hustlers, pimps & runaway gutter punks.
Most of the residents of the real *Hollywood*
are invisible immigrants,
living in Thai Town and Little Armenia
amidst sweet and sour carne asada, fried rice and falafels.
Tattoo Parlors, Strip Clubs & Wig Shops.
From well written plots to seductive sexpots,
Apartment blocks to mansion hilltops,
If you connect the dots it all spells Hollywood.

Young actors hang in the bars off Cahuenga,
shot callers & executives live up in the hills
by Mulholland,
Blue collar teamsters run behind the scenes,
Harley Davidson's, Flannels & Jeans.
Come to Where everybody's a producer &
the only thing that matters is who's hot & who's not?
Status shots portfolio, perpetrating ego.
Quest for that pot of gold @ the end of the Rainbow,
Work those angles & You just might get yours.
Be sure to bring the tools of the trade:
Headshots, Screenplay & a resume.
Not everybody does it for the craft.

You can maintain your integrity or lose your identity.

& when you get to the crossroads,
Hang onto Your soul,
Amidst the groupies, cocaine & Rock & Roll.
James Dean & Marilyn Monroe,
Jimi Hendrix & Mae West,
Frank Sinatra & Dorothy Dandridge.
Raging Bulls & Easy Riders,
Rudolph Valentino to Leonardo Dicaprio.
On the Walk of Fame
there are too many names,
between those who succeeded & suffered in vain.
Hollywood created Vegas
& the people match the furniture.
Narcissistic stars floss cars,
amidst the glamour & glitz of the Sunset Strip.

Hollywood extends far beyond its Physical district.

Worldwide from *Harry Potter* to the *Godfather*.
Hollywood is an umbrella unto itself,
The sun comes up over Santa Monica Boulevard.
Rossmore becomes Vine,

on some days you can see the Hollywood sign.

And if you drive thru Hollywood,

You'll see bright lights above transvestites,

Celebrities eating outside,

grifters looking glassy-eyed.

Heaven & hell collide, its one helluva ride,

"Dorothy you're not in Kansas anymore,"

Revisiting Hollywood lore with a whole new twist,

Cecil B. Demille wouldn't know what hit him.

Hollywood's World of entertainment

is the American dream's ultimate painting.

it's both brilliant & tragic like Michael Jackson.

Hollywood is a myth built by madness & magic.

If you connect all the dots it all spells Hollywood.
"HOORAY FOR HOLLYWOOD"

11 GREAT MOVIES ABOUT LOS ANGELES

BLADE RUNNER

SWINGERS

CHINATOWN

CAR WASH

True Romance

Big Leibowski

Falling Down

CRASH

Barfly

STRANGE DAYS

Dogtown & Z-Boys

GANGS OF LOS ANGELES

Gangs are just like any other group of people: a social system of like-minded folks uniting together on a common mission. The ethos of a street gang are not much different than a Country Club, a gun club, a church, Al Quaeda, a sports team, a fraternity. Granted these groups have different aims, but each of these groups are made up of a group of people banding together to join forces. Gangs are basically small armies. Their existence dates back to the first human settlements.

Throughout the 20th Century gangsters have been celebrated in popular culture: Al Capone, Bugsy Siegel, the *Godfather*, *GoodFellas*, *Scarface*, the *Sopranos*, *Monster Kody*, Tookie Williams and of course gangsta rap. Much of the mystique of gangsterism revolves around getting rich quick. For impressionable youth, images of the gun-slinging gangster making the quick buck & romancing the fly women make it a far more alluring opportunity than working at McDonalds. Perhaps the most obvious message is the billboard for 50 Cent's film *Get Rich or Die Tryin*. Fiddy has a microphone in one hand & a gun in the other.

"Y'all know what's crack-a-lackin

I'm from the hood of the drivebys
& kidnappings, & car-jackings."

Snoop Dogg.

Bloods, Crips, 18th Street, *Mara Salvatrucha*. Willowbrook
Compton Watts East LA Rampart, Santanas, *Longos*, Sotel,
Sarzana, Norwalk, Pacoima, Hawaiian Gardens, Grape
Street, Korean Killers, Asian Boys, Aryan Nation, KKK,
LAPD.
The tip of the Los Angeles gang iceberg. Some are names
of gangs, others are areas overrun with gangs.
The urban landscape of Los Angeles as an urban sprawl is
much harder to police than denser metropolises. Estimates
have placed as many as 200,000 gang members within
the LA area. Black & Latin gangs are more famous but
there are plenty of Asian & Anglo gangsters. And though
many gangs are made up of poor youth there are plenty
of gangsters that grew up in middle class households that
have joined for a sense of community & a variety of other
reasons.
I knew gangsters that had nicer houses than I did & brand
new Acuras the day they turned 16. For these kids its the
mystique of being a gangster. They want the perks of be
ing a gangster, like the ca$h & the women. For kids from
broken homes, gangs provide a sense of belonging or peer
support. Whereas many kids growing up in impoverished
areas like Compton or East LA join gangs as a part of
neighborhood survival. Within the inner city landscape
there is intense competition for jobs, housing & scarce pub
lic resources. In these cutthroat areas there is often little
choice.

As Mike Davis reports in the *City of Quartz*, the first black gangs in Watts were a response to the Ku Klux Klan, the LAPD & white working-class gangs living in adjacent South Gate & Huntington Park. Until the mid 1960s, Alameda Boulevard was a dividing line between the Black & White world. West of Alameda was Watts & the Black world. East of Alameda, were White working class suburbs. During the 40s, 50s & early 60s youth from both sides battled incessantly. The first Latin gangs in East LA were the Zoot Suiters who eventually fought with military personnel during the 2nd World War, otherwise known as the Zoot Suit Riots...

Many of the first gangsters of Los Angeles were clans of youth organized to defend themselves from racism & discrimination. There has always been a certain sense of lawlessness in the city of angels. The LAPD has been treating the local population like kings for well over 100 years.

After the Black Panthers dissolved in the early 70s the first Crips appeared. But what made the gangs of Los Angeles gain international notoriety was the appearance of crack cocaine in the 80s. This highly addictive toxin also has the highest profit margin. Once gangsters saw the loot they could make from crack, that is when the violence started to sky rocket. Crack not only ravaged the ghetto, but made the crack dealers vicious killers willing to do anything to protect their turf.

Murder! From the early days of Reagan through the late 1980s all the way to the 1992 Riots is generally considered the worst time period of gang violence. The 90s were much quieter all the way until a few years back in 2002 when the number of homicides (600+) was almost twice the figure seen throughout the last decade.

The post-riot unity faded away & gave way to the tense conditions that spawned gang warfare & the uprisings in the first place. The biggest factor is simple economics. Between rising gas prices & record numbers of layoffs it's not getting any better. When there are no jobs people have lots of time on their hands. The devil will find work for idle hands to do. Socioeconomic conditions keep gangs alive. Desperation fuels the gangs of Los Angeles.

There have been very few attempts to write hopeful and
optimistic visions for the future of youth involved in gangs.
One of the few that have is Luis Rodriguez. His biographi
cal novel, *Always Running: Gang Days in LA*, tells his
journey from East LA gangster to published poet to best
selling author.
Over the years he's worked with thousands of troubled youth in schools, churches, jails and prisons. His insight into their lives has made him one of the few leaders that can reach them.

In his recent book, *Hearts & Hands: Creating Community in Violent Times,* he writes.
"A community must think before attempting to shape the behavior of young people. If we treat people like animals, for the most part they will act this way. If we treat people with respect, patience, caring-being firm and consistent or flexible and open as needed-they will more likely respond in the same way. Treat people as you want to be treated."

To get much more information check the work of
Alejandro Alonso
www.streetgangs.com
&
TOM HAYDEN'S
STREET WARS

GRAFFITI WRITERS!

"In 2006, Graffiti's influence can be seen everywhere: music, clothing, video games, movies, thousands of logos, and even a company dedicated to producing spraypaint just for the art. True graffiti is not like traditional art which can be imitated. Although it is practiced and seen all around the world the way you gain respect is always the same, its all about getting up. You don't pick graffiti, it picks you."
The words above are from a young-up-and-coming art ist from Long Beach named *Motion*. Graffiti is an often misunderstood art form. It first came to mainstream atten tion in the late 1970's & 80's when films like *Beat Street*, *Style Wars* & early hip-hop became popular. In New York the writers got up on trains, in Los Angeles it was freeway overpasses & the riverbed. Some places that they hit are incredibly dangerous. Diehard writers risk their lives to get their tags up on towering billboards and sloping bridges. For the record, graffiti "writers" are different than gang sters. Though there are gangsters that write graffiti, most of the graffiti writers are edgy young individuals that need an outlet to express themselves. They are called "Writers," because they write graffiti. Basquait Keith Haring Phase 2 Doze Green Futura Chaz Mear YEM Banski Size Saber, the writers that have become famous were all driven by this need to deliver their message.
Writers know the geography of the city like a cop utilizing little known back alleys & side cuts to express their craft. LA graff legend *Mear One* writes,

"*Writers, we called our selves,*
Silent warriors whose identity remained at home.
Strange new breed,
The initiation of a youth into graffitist is a
mythological path."

Dating back to the cave dwellers, Graffiti is easily the
earliest urban art form. It is immediate, it is the moment. A visual
scream. The term "graffiti" comes from the Italian word "*graffiare.*"
Graffiare means "to scratch." By scratching their words and images
on walls, graffiti artists are
active participants in a material world. By asserting their art they are
manifesting their vision instantly. This timeless act has been used to
make political statements, woo a lover, celebrate one's self or claim
gang territory.
Graffiti is as timeless as oral storytelling. Mear One shares,

"Speak the oldest language, and paint
Paint as the ancestors did
From cave walls to toilet stalls
we kept the language alive."

Los Angeles graffiti crews come from every neighborhood.
Koreatown, Palms, Hancock Park, Venice, East Hollywood, the
Valley, Long Beach. Kids of all races. Crews like SH, AMSEVEN, CBS
Can't Be Stopped. NASA, KBH, UTI, MSK, WCA, LA BOMB
SQUAD, K2S. As big as LA is, kids know each other from east to west,
north Hollywood, downtown to Venice. Young graff writers know
about their peers. Everybody knows who's getting up. Legends are
made. Packs of roving writers roam the city.
A few legends have died in the act.
The legendary west coast pioneer *Chaz* cut his teeth painting in the
tunnels of Highland Park. He told me, "You need to spend a mini-
mum of 10 years in the street to call yourself a graffiti writer. You
have to make a choice if it's really that important." The risks involved
with being a graffiti
artist make it inherently a challenging act. The graffiti subculture is
one where you need to respect the codes to gain respect. He notes, "I
did graffiti by myself for 20 years, an artist is a lifestyle, a true painter
is a worker."

The very best writers seem to be the ones who hold it as a sacred act. The legendary late Sk8 felt "graffiti was a vehicle for change." Whether or not you believe graffiti is art, it is a rapidly growing art form & has been around since the dawn of man. Mear One.

"The woman with one eye
at Sunset & Alvarado
keeps coming with no clue,
searching, ranting,
raving for a better life
& no ones listening,
so I re-iterate;
there is a message painted on a wall
in a neighborhood near you
And it states
'GRAFFITI IS THE VOICE
OF THE DISSATISFIED SOUL!"

Writers write,
write the night
invisible to sight brighter than bright!
Write the light…

On a wall near you!
A new book on the history of L.A. graffiti art just dropped…
www.thehistoryoflosangelesgraffitiart.com.

The Emperor Wears No Clothes

Take a short walk with me
into the world of fashion.
Vogue Cosmopolitan Mademoiselle
Peasant wear handcrafted *couture,*
Ziou Zsa Zsa fashion faux paux,
Forty-something mamas charge cards. They charge large from Prada
to Bogota Versace to Liberace,
Maharishi to Cavaricci,
zenith to zeitgeist,
Cashmere to fleece, Park Avenue to the Swap Meet
look-alike couples & fashionistas.
Rolling in like supermodels,
Spoiled kids coddled holding a little ass dog. Drama queens, fashion
magazines, your grill On the big screen,
Paparazzi people
blinded by bizarro
worshipping a world built by the barrio…
The quest for power makes people ugly, ruthless ambition
guided by social climbing & profit margins.
Greedy values strip people of soulfullness
Creating zombies.
Hypocrites with an exaggerated
sense of self importance.
Some people get a little clout &
forget where they came from.
the kind of people that'll make a mess
& then ask you to clean it up.
Like the wealthy wanna look like the *proletariat.*
Old styles once worthless always resurface.
The world of fashion is populated by pretenders
afraid to know themselves.

In the city of fantasy too many ignore reality.
Its easy when you can hop into your SUV under palm
trees. But not everybody is a celebrity, for every VIP,
There's at least two or three that feed the children
Or pick up the dry cleaning.

They're the fabulous fashionistas,
zipper zapatistas, celebrity sandistas.
Topanga trustafarians
are sipping soy milk in the canyon.
Cocaine caffeine wheatgrass ginseng
royal jelly *Echinacea* Red Bull!
The world has been thrusted into turbo
& people are losing their souls turning to chemicals.
Bourgeois bohemians drinking espresso
turn their nose up at the ghetto
But wanna be ghetto fabulous at Fred Segal.
Is it irony, hypocrisy, how about gluttony?
How much food can a fat man eat?
They aspire to acquire, a culture based on desire,
The desire to inspire & share got replaced with bad hair,
Greed & vanity, the 7 deadly sins of humanity
The blurring of fantasy & reality,
$7000 shopping sprees & landscapes of Disney.
Get your $500 jeans across the street
from starving families, The emperor wears no clothes.
They call 'em thrift stores off Highland
& vintage Down on Melrose.
It's getting hot in here,
So take off all your clothes
& join in celebration of
Skin, sin & hedonism.
Live from the Playboy Mansion.
People are dancing.
The emperor wears no clothes.

What is Silverlake?

Silverlake is where Century old shrubs
hug cascading hills, case study houses
host well cooked meals.
A home for multicultural, alternative lifestyles,
body art after dark,
Akbar, double parked cars.
Retro throwback with futuristic culture clash.

Silverlake is body piercing,
vintage chic, fashionably dirty.
A place of tolerant machismo,
irie sessions in wooded bungalows.

Silverlake is Tantric conquistadors,
acoustic electronica,
Jerk chicken, cold coronas, lipstick lesbians,
dysfunctional divas, staircases at Micheltorena,
club scensters, garage bands, El Cid, the Spaceland,
Soundlessons & I & I Productions.
Silverlake is Stonesthrow, Kajmere Sound, transsexual
swan songs, nocturnal neon above chess players all night
long. It's another funky function,
Silverlake Sunset Junction.
Between Motown & London, Bangkok & Mexico City,
Silverlake is gritty & cosmopolitan.
Another side of Los Angeles not as celebrated
as Beverly Hills Baywatch.
Glitter tops, birkenstocks, dreadlocks & headshots.
Ghetto glamorous on the *eastside* of Hollywood.
Silverlake is shaggy hair, sun hats,
trucker caps, chain wallets, skaters,
mullets, Red Hot Chili Peppers, Beck,
Jurassic 5, Jane's Addiction, Ozomatli,

Rage Against the Machine. Black Eyed Peas, Leo D,
black glasses, goatees, gothic teens,
vegan cuisine,clove cigarettes, hilltop crosses,
an Alternative Press & PBS Broadcasts.
Where else but Silverlake
would the *Body Mind Spirit Center*
be upstairs from porn in the Circus of Books?
Take a look—it's Silverlake!
God rest Elliot Smith at Solutions.
Silverlake is a Conservatory of Music,
home of artsy foreign flicks
& tasty Kitchen eating.

Silverlake is a Mecca for art & freedom…

WEBS OF PARALLEL EXISTENCE

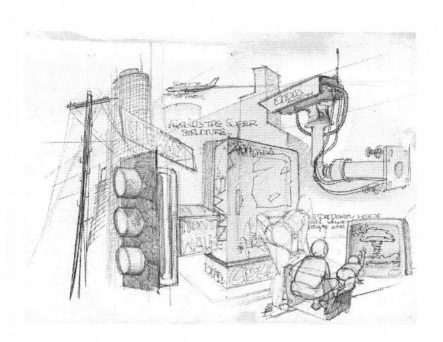

Every year Silverlake has the two-day Sunset Junction street festival.

I wrote this hanging at the Junction for two days.

Sunset Junction

There goes the girl with the dog again.

I saw Saul Williams, Blackbird, 7 &
Sam Humphries. Sedated junkies jammed
the streets were slammed,
seductive scented women
wound around our stand,
Kajmere Sound recordings.

Silverlake Sunset Junction Atwater Village
Echo Park chillin'.
I got my groove back with record stacks
red stripes, a warm night, irie flights,
tanned, toned & tight
the music so right,
kickin' Cali livin'.
Dr. Oop, Aztech Sol, Dusk,
B+, Shippy, Yuki, Abstract Rude,
Frowhawk 2-Feathers, Art, Emi, Loslito, Hiro,
I love my people.

France has a city named Paris,
that dude McCristoll's last names' Harris.
The door in the back is seldom locked,
hot hot heat came outta Chris Haycock.
The block got hot, there were a grip of cops,
Arthur Lee & Love played the main stage,
We stayed under a vine garden in an
inverted back patio below shadows.
"I don't take requests," We stay blessed,
Witness the meeting of heavyweights
"yeah baby go on & have some fun,"
Ubiquity Sound sessions
Los Angeles lounge lessons
Let's listen.

Scion Root Down Dodger fans
W. Bush got red, people smiled
& a grip of rough riders flamed fire fighters
below Buck Fush, chronic Kush,
Anti-Bush *Impeach the Precedent*,
Silverlake residents live alternative lifestyles
so many smiles 'cuz it keeps getting better.

Music!

"Surf naked,"
"Books not Bombs."
"Vagina is for lovers,"
"Ca$h from chaos"
When it gets dark,
it usually gets wild,
Music. Soul. Child.

Musical children got wild
jamming with Flea & Lonnie Marshall,
their weapon of choice is to use their voice
at the *Silverlake Conservatory of Music*.
B. Pope, Azul,
2 cool ass fools
opened up their space
so we could parlay on a bangin' ass Sunday.
A day I needed to hang back & collect my thoughts,
"it feels like the music
sounds better with you."
Everyone hung.
Artists, musicians, poets, djs,
partygoers, celebrities & nobodies.
The nobodies are celebrities & music is everything.

Toasts were offered all around,
we hanging in the background
There's a big ass backyard at the Upon Shop.
Fresh Air came from Khalil,
Fat Al was on the wheels,
a vibe so cool, people volunteered to
be the happy helper.

Sno cones came outta the ice machine,
B. Pope laced it clean,
what a day it's been.
Never quitters, straight heavy hitters
we're blessed to be here,
all of us are a cionados,
Rashida mixes awesome.
House music all night long,
she mixes cleaner than the bald dude,
Compu Sol, dancehall.

The sign on the wall
says, "So many times it happens too fast
you trade your passion for glory,"

That isn't our story,
Common into Tribe
is more my vibe,
The streets are alive,
This ish is niice,
the baby sways left to right,
it's a beautiful night,
Love me or leave me alone,
the poem is my home.

The sun, the moon, the stars,
We got outta our cars
& danced on the boulevard!

Secret Streets

Thousands of square miles of concrete connect commuters through LA's built environment. Boulevards like Sunset, Wilshire, Ventura and Figueroa are world famous. For lo cals, they are even more famous for the traffic. Congestion has led local commuting veterans to determine the fastest routes to circumvent gridlock. Through a lot of trial and er ror enlightened drivers find more low profile thoroughfares that get them where they need to go much faster. There are hundreds of valuable shortcuts embedded deep in the urban fabric. Here are 10 streets that can save you a lot of time when there's traffic. Secret streets for the Valley and South Bay aren't included in this piece only because the city is too big.

Wilton/Arlington/Van Ness: This road goes uninterrupted from Torrance all the way to the Hollywood Hills.
At Slauson, Van Ness becomes Arlington. At Olympic, Arlington becomes Wilton. It's still the same road the whole way. This artery is far faster than Western or Normandie & undercover for 20+ miles.

Hauser: Hauser goes from the Crenshaw District to Miracle Mile in quiet style. It beats La Brea or Fairfax.
Inglewood Blvd: Inglewood Blvd begins in Mar Vista and goes all the way to Florence Blvd in Inglewood. It's a great alternative to the 405 or Sepulveda. The name changes to Centinela at Jefferson, but it's the same street for 10+ miles.
Palms: One of the best of the best. Palms goes from Venice to Pico-Robertson passing through Mar Vista, Palms and Cheviot Hills. Compared to Pico or Venice, Palms is the real deal.

23rd/Walgrove: Passing just west of the Santa Monica airport, this north south slide is a smooth sloped ride when Westside roads like Lincoln or Bundy/Centinela are hellish.

Buckingham: When you need to get from the Crenshaw district to midcity, Buckingham is much quicker than Crenshaw. It connects to West Blvd and a funky scenic bridge close to Washington.

Ocean Park: This is by far the quietest east-west artery in SANTA Monica.

6th Street: Though 6th gets hectic in Koreatown, it goes from East LA to Fairfax pretty fast and it's beautiful through Hancock Park.

Allesandro: This small road goes from Echo Park over to Riverside Drive and Elysian Valley far faster than Glendale Blvd.

San Vicente: It's 2 portions are both diagonal forces, the eastern portion goes from midcity to the top of the Sunset Strip.

The Brentwood portion of San Vicente has very few stop lights after Bundy. You can coast quickly all the way to the water in Santa Monica.

Every neighborhood has these roads. The value of these secret streets is how much faster they are than usual suspects like La Brea or Wilshire. Explore a bit more and you might be surprised how much time you can save.

Knowledge is earned & the time you save is yours.

DENSITY

Density entwines webs
of parallel existence
thick in the heart
of the inner city.
Parallel webs of existence
mix thick in the dense mosaic.
Endless characters coexist
on the long list: students,
socialists, tourists, fundamentalists,
sado-masochists, actresses, pimps,
press agents, company presidents,
lesbians burning incense
there's endless residents.
Screenwriters, fly-by-nighters,
gamblers, grifters so many scene shifters
hustlers, house wives, shoplifters,
quick cash seekers, judicial readers,
attendants checking parking meters,
bums drinking liters, old men in wife beaters.
These are the comical leaders
of urban fable sharing the air
in the beautiful built environment
we call Los Angeles.

Density entwines webs
of parallel existence
thick in the heart
of the inner city.

Westside 'wood rats
old folks crossing Fairfax
past drive-through check cash
Lakeside spatial mismatch
Culver green cross backs
the multi-cultural people mass
keeps inching along urban arteries
this is density-density
congesting mid-city karaokes
around Alvarado fake ID's
39 cents at Mickey-D's
the bus benches frontin' Frosty's Freeze
seeing Washington Socrates
bicycling Ballona Creek to Venice Beach-

Density! Density entwines webs of parallel existence
thick in the heart of the inner city.

Bouncing back Banana Bungalow
achieving archipelagoes
past Palisade fern grottos
as the panoramic fronds of palms
are calming Tom Collins
Who's Sunset Strip sipping?
The neon super semiotics
punctuates the power of place
in the distinctive social space
you call your own home-
deciphering diction in
the landscape vernacular.

Density entwines webs
of parallel existence
thick in the heart of the inner city

Buildings.

There are some incredible structures in Southern California. Not only do I love architecture, but I like the way buildings blend with the landscape, otherwise known as the built environment. Here are 10 of my favorite building/structures in no particular order.

Wiltern Theater @ Wilshire & Western
Binocular Building in Santa Monica off Main Street
El Capitan Theater on Hollywood Blvd.
Bradbury Building in downtown on Broadway
Royce Hall—UCLA
Downtown Central Library
Watts Towers
Bullocks Wilshire
Los Angeles Theatre on Braodway & 6th
4th Street Bridge

Other favorite locations

Carroll Avenue—Angelino Heights
Point Fermin—San Pedro
Signal Hill—Central Long Beach
Barnsdall Art Park—East Hollywood/Los Feliz

Roads of Thunder:

The biggest of the big boulevards.
These roads move a lot of cars…

Wilshire: Downtown to the Ocean. MacArthur Park, Koreatown, Miracle Mile, Beverly Hills, UCLA.

Olympic: Always faster than Wilshire, one of the widest boulevards in the city.

Ventura: The Valley's Wilshire. Studio City to Calabasas, coffee anyone?

Sepulveda: LA's longest street goes from the Deep Valley West LA, South Bay into the LBC.

Crenshaw: Take the 'Shaw all the way to Torrance. It starts at Wilshire.

La Brea/Hawthorne Blvd: Hollywood Inglewood Rancho Palos Verdes, what else do you want?

Venice Blvd: At times it may be the fastest street in Los Angeles.
LA Cienega: Hillside Fast as a freeway, LAX a quieter way on a lucky day.

Vermont: Los Feliz to San Pedro, straight as an arrow.

Western: Hollywood Hills to Palos Verdes, the straightest line of street lights.

Slauson: Industrial on the eastside by the River, you can take it all the way to the Marina.

WILSHIRE WORDS

WHAT IS IT ABOUT WILSHIRE

THAT MAKES IT THE EQUATOR

OF OUR FAIR CITY?

IS IT THE BERLIN WALL

OF BEVERLY HILLS

& SOUTH CITY?

THE GREAT WALL OF

HOUSEKEEPERS &

PORCELAIN PRETTY?

WILSHIRE IS GLAMOROUS

& GRITTY, QUINTESSENTIAL

ALL CITY…

IT PERSONIFIES ALL
THAT IS LOS ANGELES!

Pockets of people
pack the boulevard
cars cars cars.
Monuments & mendicants
mix on Wilshire,
single room occupants
keep moving.
The itinerant immigrants
works Wilshire as it's
lifeblood.
Wilshire is it's source.
the rapidly moving artery
in the city's big body
All aboard!!
Cops & Protestants,
fake i-d's & intoxicants,
transplants & land grants
Wilshire's plan enchants
the populace.
A smorgasbord of
textures & sensations.
Flavors,
architecture, culture.
Wilshire is a river
like the Nile
or Mississippi.
Massive!!
Wilshire is a small
galaxy of Villages,
pockets, neighborhoods.
Is it Rampart Koreatown
or Historic Filipinotown?

One Wilshire
MacArthur Park
Pico Union
MTA west to Western
Old jazz musicians who
played at the *Cocoanut Grove*
used to drink early at
the H.M.S. Bounty.
Park Mile extends out
of Koreatown
I walked down Wilshire
on stretches east of Crenshaw
glad to be on the boulevard.
one man in a sea of cars.
the big old buildings make
me feel small, concrete canyons
glass & steel.
Wilshire is where fathers & sons
drove to talk about the world
the speedway opens up
past Beverly Hills
ask Christian Slater & Axl Rose.
All aboard: Wilshire!!
Wilshire is where
dreams are made
& tragedy plays
side by side.
Hundred thousand
dollar car$ wait at
red lights right
next to guys panhandling
on the side
sitting on the busstop.

Green light & their off
but for just a second
their energy intersects.
Wilshire is the crossroads!

213 323 310.

Three different area codes,

taco trucks & TV episodes

Wilshire explodes art deco

skyscraper boulevard

all the way to the ocean

about 16 miles.

Wilshire Words

there aren't enough

words for Wilshire.

Part 2.

The street that married
us damn near buried us,
Wilshire is where it
all started.
She lived a block north
of me off 6th & St. Andrews.
I was on St. Andrews
close to 7th.
We met at Wilshire
in the middle.
Interracial lovers
& racist gangsters
crystallize vibes
on street corners.
We started hanging out
once we discovered
how close
our places were.
Sooner than later
she was living with me.
& They say relationships
can be affected by geography?
We lived in a small apartment
with not enough money
& not enough patience
or capacity to even stand
a chance of lasting.
Lodged between Wilshire
& 6th, the Versailles Apartments
where we lived
was also the home of
James Ellroy in his work *My Dark Places*.

She had a New York
State of mind
on California time,
an eager beaver in
a bread line,
equipped with a mind
too fast for public transit,
Wilshire went slow,
then fast,
she couldn't stand it.

On the night of one
of our last fights
you left me at the *Temple Bar*
you took the car
& I walked down Wilshire
you found me 20 minutes later,
I was damn near to West LA,
I almost caught the MTA.
You wouldn't let
me get away.

5 *L.A. Views*

ANGELES NATIONAL FOREST

High above the smog line
amongst the manzanita & medusa
the Angeles national forest looms lush
& green after last year's heavy rain.
A few cars on the road below
occasionally break
the mountain's silence.

A deep forest of green
gives good energy to all
urban warriors that visit.
Here's a whole other side
of Los Angeles County,
after all it is the
Angeles National Forest.

Most Angelenos
don't even know
how beautiful it is
above the metropolis.

There are still a few folks
who know the intricacies
of a mountain's landscape
like the Earth people did.
To know the Earth around you
with intimate understanding
is to really be alive.

Rainbows in the cloud,
pink & purple light
from the sky reflects
on the pines
in the marathon of this life
nature overtakes us,
let the clouds roll in &
buckle down,
the sky holds multitudes.
Birds, clouds, moisture.
Feel the shifts in the wind
as the sunset begins
the sky is electric,
high clouds are bigger than
the biggest battleships.
Raw Earth
heals the spirit
I let the mountains seep
into my skin.
Spotted colors keep
the consciousness
connected to the road ahead.
The second wave of light
got Strawberry Peak
glowing above fog &
it looks better than Mars.
Sandcastle clouds drip
moisture like cold winds
call nights arrival,
the last two red stripes
catch purple underlight.
Electric peach is neon plum
the earth & sun are one,
I bow to the sunset, *Beautiful...*

LONG BEACH BLUES

I've heard folks call the Metro Blue Line between Long Beach and Los Angeles "the Dirty Train."

It's more like a pipeline through sacred terrain too often forgotten. In a world of California rolls and BMW's, many people are ignorant of how the other half lives.

The Blue Line slices through some of the most fascinating areas of the Southland. It offers a candid portrait of life you'd never see on the freeways starting from Downtown L.A. through South Central into industrial Vernon, Willowbrook, Compton, Rancho Dominguez and Carson on the way to Downtown Long Beach.

Southern California once had a public transportation sys tem of trains as extensive as the New York City Subway system. Known as the Pacific Electric Streetcar, it had over 1,000 miles of tracks looping from the San Fernando Valley to Newport Beach, Venice to Claremont and everywhere in between.

The legendary lines had colorful names like *The Balloon Route* and *The Triangle Trolley.*

My grandfather told me stories of riding the streetcars dur ing the Depression. He would ride the train to Broadway to see movies for a nickel or out to the beach in Santa Monica. As cars became more popular the streetcars were no longer profitable and were phased out. Conspiracy theorists point to the Oil industry and major Car manufacturers as the cause. For more info on this check the film *Who Framed Roger Rabbit?*

Flash forward to the start of the 21st Century.
Automobile traffic has become ridiculous.
Policy leaders realize trains are a great option for public transportation. They decide to build a light rail train between Los Angeles and Long Beach following the old Pacific Electric right-of-way.

This light rail is the Metro Blue Line. Finished in 1990, the ridership has followed a steady upward trend.

I boarded the train at 7P.M. in Downtown L.A. at the 7th and Metro Station. Amidst the rush of people are nurses still in uniform, downtown office workers, cops checking your ticket, traveling mariachi musicians, students and mothers of every race and color holding bicycles, backpacks, briefcases, leather purses, headphones, bandannas and baby carriages.

The lifeblood of our city!
What follows are visions out of a moving window. The train begins underground emerging out of the tunnel next to Staples Center on Flower Street. The first stop is Pico. Through my window the sun slowly sets over the arena's sleek silver facade. We're off!

Zipping past parking lots, cheap hotels, commercial printers, freeway entrances and medical clinics. Billboards, graffiti and bricks. Between stops stretch the streets of inner-city Los Angeles.

The train winds left into Washington Boulevard heading east. We're descending deep into L.A.'s underbelly.
Street signs barrage me: Mufflers shops, Mariscos, Public Storage, Factories.

The train cuts south on industrial stretch of Long Beach Avenue.
Long Beach here we come!

My excitement is matched by the cries of the baby behind me. Meanwhile two seats away two tired workers keep sleeping. These two cats are so tired they could sleep
through anything.

In the Alameda Corridor it's nothing but catwalks, pub
lic storage facilities, rows of 20-feet high stacked wood
pallets, junkyards and cargo trains. The train elevates 50
feet up or so north of Slauson. Below are brown logs and
cranes.

We zip back down past small houses with chipped paint. Dried, palm fronds blow in the breeze. Blowing by Florence, Firestone and Century past small parks with baseball games and lovers sitting in the shade.

At the 103rd Station a sign announces the construction of the Wattstar Theater and Education Center. It is a desperately needed facility for the area. Barry White grew up in Willowbrook near here. How many babies were made because of that man? He was a man of his community, continuing his loyalty even after his fame. The City of Los Angeles recently changed the name of nearby South Park Recreation Center to the *Barry White Recreation Center.*

Just before the Imperial Station and the 105 Freeway, the Watts Towers loom a few hundred yards west. A monument built of scrap metal and bottle caps by Italian immigrant Simon Rodia that took nearly 30 years.

Up next is Compton. A city founded nearly a century ago as a Methodist community. George W. Bush lived here in his early childhood. His father worked nearby in the oil industry. Passing the Artesia Station teenage shot callers talk on their cell phones. Compton is known as the birthplace of gangsta rap, In spite of all the hype, it is a bedroom community of modest homes.

We pass over the Los Angeles River, the Blue Line Maintenance yard and into North Long Beach approaching Del Amo. Words on a wall past Willow read, "WWW means World Wide Woe."
Soon we are on Long Beach Boulevard and the train is no longer full. Some guy behind me tells a girl across the aisle, "I hope your boyfriend makes you happy, if he doesn't call me soon."

It's 7:50 P.M. and we're almost there. Exiting at Pine and 1st Street a smiling bandolero in a cowboy hat hugs his waiting wife. The warmth from their tender embrace puts a smile on my face, it's been a majestic ride. I walk into Rock Bottom Brewery feeling electric, bring on the night!

BUTTER & GOLD

Riding the Gold Line offers an intimacy with the landscape not possible in a car. It's a journey through wooded chaparral, craftsman architecture and multicultural Los Angeles. Downtown LOS Angeles to Pasadena.
A view so close, you can see in people's backyards. It starts in the shadows of the Downtown skyscrapers at Union Station.
At 6:30 P.M. the train is full with tired workers reading, sightseers, young lovers and every breed of Angeleno. First up is Chinatown.

The original Chinatown was the city's vice district, known
for having underground tunnels housing opium dens, gam
bling and prostitution. It was located on the present site of
Union Station before being relocated a half-mile northwest
in the 1930s.

Chinatown now has art galleries on Chung King Way and funky night life @ "Hop Louie" and "Firecracker." Directly east are factories with Chinese characters, yards of school buses, County U.S.C. Hospital, freeway bridges, walls of graffiti and the concrete channel called the L.A. River.

Next is Lincoln Heights/Cypress Park. Passengers talk
excitedly about their work day. An anti-graffiti poster in the train reads,
"Limpia Los Angeles."

Passing Pentecostal churches, the train enters the Arroyo Seco, which means "dry creek." This is a lush region of
oaks, sycamores, eucalyptus and rustic houses along the small water-way running from Pasadena to Elysian Park. The Gold Line and 110 zigzag one another through hillside communities like Montecito Heights, Mt. Washington, Highland Park, Garvanza and South Pasadena. These communities are charming and underappreciated. Heritage Square has several exquisite 19th Century Victorian houses relocated from Bunker Hill, artifacts dating back to before the down-town skyscrapers were built.

The Southwest Museum, founded by Charles Fletcher Lummis was the first museum ever built in Los Angeles. It celebrates the indige-nous residents of the Arroyo Seco.

During the 1890's the Arroyo Seco was a bastion for the Arts and Crafts Movement. Home to architects, poets, painters and musi-cians, L.A.'s first art movement. Lummis was the patriarch. He walked to L.A. from Ohio in the 1880's and served as the L.A. Times first City Editor.

It's by no coincidence Mt. Washington and Highland Park are our-ishing art communities today because this dates back to the arts and crafts legacy of Lummis.

The train slows down in Highland Park. Children play
dodge ball in their yards. At the Mission Station signs read,
"No Horn Bells!" In South Pasadena the houses are impres
sive and the foliage gets denser. White-collar riders exit.
Iron work sculpture on the gates of the Del Mar station
intrigues young art students. This stop is for shoppers and
bar hoppers.
Old Town Pasadena!

The Gold Line ends in Sierra Madre as the train emerges in
the center of the 210 freeway. Cars speed by on both sides
and a purple glow in the sky makes for another nuclear
sunset.
Zooming just below the base of Mount Wilson and the San Gabriel
Mountains, the lights of the San Gabriel Valley lie below and the
Gold Line races on.

6 NOTHING MATTERS

BUT THE MUSIC

ROOT DOWN SOUND.

Make no mistake,
there is no sound in town
like the mighty Root Down!

DJ Dusk let's us know every Thursday @ Los Angeles'
legendary hip-hop, funk and soul club, known as *The Root
Down*. In the world of historic weekly parties there are few
that have the legacy of the Root Down. The weekly soiree
featuring Dusk, *Loslito, Musicman Miles & Wyatt Case* is
now in its eighth year. The original formula has been so
successful that it has two monthly satellite clubs in Costa
Mesa, CA (Orange County), and New York City. Over
the years, the Root Down opened the door and provided a
platform for emerging superstars like *Jurassic 5,* Dilated
Peoples, Black Eyed Peas, Freestyle Fellowship, *Crown
City Rockers, Visionaries,* Cut Chemist, Nu-Mark & DJ
Shadow. Not only have many luminaries passed through the
Root Down but two monster bands and a record label have
grown out of it's foundation: *The Rebirth, Breakestra &
Kajmere Sound.* Founders Miles Tackett & Carlos "Loslito"
Guaico started it as a jam session @ a coffeehouse back in
1996. The called it *The Breaks*, because that's what they
played. A collection of the best local players congregated to
jam. Live players, emcees & dancers. Cats like Cut Chem
ist & Mixmaster Wolf had paved the way with their *Peace
Pipe*, event in the early 90s.
The house band of the Breaks became the *Breakestra*.
Founded by Tackett, the Breakestra has always been a
who's who of local bad asses. The only two members from the begin-
ning that have remained constant are bassist/guitarist/upright cel-
list/producer/vocalist Tackett and vocalist Mixmaster Wolf.

Critical players over the years include Josh Cohen on drums, Chris "C-Qwest," Taylor also on drums, Geoff "Double G," Gallegos on sax and ute, funk free agent Todd Simon and Paul Vargas on trumpet, Dan Osterman on trombone, Carlos Guaico on keys, Davy Chegwidden on percussion and Dan Ubick on guitar. "Playing in the Breakestra is a great way to get your de gree in funk," says Loslito. Graduates that currently hold a coveted Breakestra degree have gone on to start their own projects, including Loslito with the Rebirth, Double G with *Dakah Hip-Hop Orchestra* and Ubick with *Connie Price and the Keystones*. Simultaneously both Peanut Butter Wolf and Egon from *Stonesthrow Records* were both long time members of the Root Down Soundsystem since the late 90s. In 2001 Breakestra's album *Live Mix Part 2,* came out on Stonesthrow. The Root Down has a lot of talent getting down in one space. Like Dusk says, "We're celebrating life tonight!"

As this book went to press, DJ Dusk tragically passed on 4-29-06. His powerful spirit was the heart & soul of the Root Down. Dusk's great djing & poignant words made him a true legend. Dusk was truly alive in Los Angeles. We will miss his giant spirit.

The rotating evolution of both the Root Down and the Breakestra has inspired an incredible whirlwind of cre ativity. The Root Down is still going strong after 8 years. Breakestra closed out 2005 by releasing "Hit the Floor," on Ubiquity, it's their first album of original songs & it is swinging.

The entire time Loslito played with Breakestra, he was writing original compositions and arrangements. The Rebirth have been jamming together since the mid 90's. It took 'em 7 years for their recent debut album, "This Journey In," Loslito explains, "You make records to stand the test of time, so you craft it until it feels right." *Mambo's*

Cuban Restaurant was one of the focal points where players would meet. Ralph "Lil Big Fat" Gonzalez' family serves up incredible Cuban food. Jam sessions would be accompanied by some very tasty plantains.

The Rebirth's label *Kajmere Sound* grew out of gatherings @ Mambo's. Loslito met the eventual Kajmere C.E.O. Joseph Davidian there as well. Davidian was a musician himself. Los invited him out to the Root Down and David ian immediately dug the funk & soul of the weekly party. Before he knew it they got together with Charles Raggio, a veteran of the music scene and the rest is history. The ethos of MAMBO'S Cuban food and ambiance ts the funk & soul sounds of not only the Rebirth but Kajmere Sound's whole vibe. Loslito shares, "We are not afraid to explore all the world's rhythms and incorporate our individual in u ences. The challenge is to try to make it all work together and give it a new spin."

The Rebirth's debut album, *This Journey In*, was nominated in 2005 by BBC and Gilles Peterson for Album of the Year. Their classic soul with a futuristic twist is infectious. The point for them according to Loslito, "is to bring back the classic family soul band like Earth, Wind & Fire or Kool & the Gang." The Rebirth is accomplishing this with their 7-piece unit that includes Patrick Bailey on guitar, Greg Malone on bass, Noelle Scaggs on lead vocals, Mark Cross on keys, Chris Taylor on drums, Ralph Gonzalez on percussions & Loslito on keys & vocals. They closed out the year with an epic show at the Natural History Museum with *Rocky Dawuni*.

Speaking of Rocky Dawuni, the man is an incredible songwriter. The Ghana Native splits his time between Los Angeles & Africa. His music is somewhere fuses afrobeat, reggae, hip-hop, hi-life & turntablism. His album *Book of Changes*, is original but feels like you've heard it before. It has that timeless feel.

Rocky hosts the weekly club *Afro Funke* @ Zanzibar in Santa Monica. It's an evening dedicated to African funksoul music. When Rocky began imagining the vibe he hand picked DJ *Jeremy Sole* to be the primary sound selector. Rocky told me in 2003 that Jeremy "is the best dj in LA and nobody knows about him." Not anymore. Over the last few years Afro Funke has become legendary in nightlife folklore. In November 2004 the man who is known to the world as STEVIE WONDER, was actually on stage at Afro Funke listening to Zap Mama as she had her album release party at Afro Funke. Rocky befriended Stevie a few summers ago in Ghana and they've been hooking up since.

Jeremy Sole wrote these words about it:
"Stevie's beloved smile and head rocking was increasing
with every beat. The capacity crowd was raging with joy,
reveling in the fact that we were in the right place at the
right time. Stevie started playing congas with Marwan,
and KCRW's Garth Trinidad took over on turntables. Zap Mama's
musicians grabbed tambourines, drums and a flute. Kadiatu was
doing traditional West African dances on
stage, while Marie beat-boxed a call and response between Marwan,
Stevie and herself. Garth finished an amazing
30-minute DJ set with the jam. I took the tables again to
keep it moving. It was midnight and people were hugging strangers
like long-lost family members. Zap Mama went down to the dance
floor to dance with everyone while Stevie spoke heart-to-heart with
no more than one or two folks at a time. 1:30am, Stevie, Zap Mama
and the rest of the
momentous family danced and hugged until last call. The
last song was "Ain't That Love" by Ray Charles, in honor of his birth-
day. Stevie grabbed the mic again and sang the whole tune with a life
of memories in every word."

DANCIN' TIMES

Los Angeles club culture is
burning like a Firecracker.

People are loving the euphoria
sweat's pouring, people bouncing
ladies scent lingers on body movement-
nothing matters but the music-
people are losing their sorrows/
dancing till tomorrow.

Strobe lights sparkle
over the ghetto glamorous all stars,
the educated partiers, the renaissance artists
the turntablists, word sages, actors,
graphic designers, musicians, dancers,
photographers, poets, promoters,
crews of club kids in the multicultural mix
it's like *fried chicken & chopsticks*-
the Los Angeles hot ish!
Who got it in the postmodern metropolis?
We rocking the populace-

People are dancing,
These are dancing times.

I walked outside of myself across the oor
feeling the bass bounce off the boards
the dancing body of the mind took shape
at the intersection of the times Sashaying
hemlines marijuana eyes promise thighs
hooked in addiction while the dj turned
tables with white labels breaking news
fables between the new age and creation

Audiovisual sensation crystal balls
video walls strobelight fantasies in
more rooms than two honeys can attach
check the mismatch
the sonic boom patch
drum & bass attacks
electronic soul hop polyrhythm PHAT!
Ladies scent lingers on body movement,
Nothing matters but the music.

People are dancing
These are dancing times

Dancin' while the music blasts,
Ladies move fast,
BOOM CRASH & FLASH!
Club culture is a crazy spectacle.
Everybody's dressed to kill in shiny material.
Hip-hop dread locks tank tops,
sweaty bras skin showing off it's hot.
You got every race, gays, straights,
multi-colors, metal eyelashes, transvestites,
transsexuals—Rugged, wild & beautiful people.
Strobelight visuals add to sensual stimulation
DJ's are playing sound creations
The new generation is finding salvation
by dancing
People are dancing,
these are dancing times!

LOS ANGELES GROWS INTO ITSELF

Five years into the 21st Century Los Angeles is transform
ing rapidly. Not only are massive demographic changes
underway, but the quintessential suburban metropolis has
become urban. With over 100 miles of coastline already
built out 100 miles inland, there's no more room for Los
Angeles to grow. The very thing the builders of this city
were trying to escape (overcrowded high-density develop
ment) has become our reality. People are everywhere. Even
outlier areas like the Inland Empire and Orange County
have become urban. The region's increase in density turns
up the thermostat a little more. It's only gonna get hot
ter. New mayor *Antonio Villaraigossa* is eager to lead the
multicultural populace. After all these years, Los Angeles is
finally growing into itself.

The real soul of Los Angeles is what's emerging. Holly
wood has shown us *Baywatch, Beverly Hills 90210, Blade
Runner* and *Boyz in the Hood*. Our endless parade of forest
fires, celebrity trials, riots, earthquakes, labor strikes and
landslides has even become old news. There are so many
LA stories that have yet to be told. The hundreds of neigh
borhoods in the city of Los Angeles are comprised of fas
cinating people from allover the world. The real flavor of
Los Angeles takes some time to get to. By digging deeper
you can find the soul of Los Angeles. It's much more subtle
than the usual stereotypes. Beyond the facades lie a vibrant
core of immigrant and artistic communities that inject new
life into the city.

The substance within the many unique communities makes up a mosaic that geographer Ed Soja says, "represents the world in connected urban microcosms." You can journey from Mexico to Korea to Iran to Thailand to Armenia in a few miles of driving. The bustling energy in these districts and the flourishing underground art movement are just two examples of authentic Los Angeles. Experiences like eating Pho at 4 in the morning or dancing on the rooftop of an afterhours party as the sun comes up epitomize the exciting spirit of 21st Century Los Angeles.

The California dream is alive and well, even as the price of real estate and gas climb into the stratosphere. Exponential growth of the area has been occurring over the last 100 years; about the same time the first automo biles were built. This defining invention was a catalyst for the rise of a new urban landscape in Southern California. LA's urban sprawl is a reflection of worldwide changes in transportation, communication and sense of time and space. This is why the builders of LA attempted to defy the traditional, high-density urban landscapes of pre-industrial, pre-technological cities.

Multi-dimensional Los Angeles, with all its faces, embodies the changing definition of a city. Being the youngest major World City, a child of contemporary culture, it's only natural that the emerging characteristics here differ from the historic urban paradigms. Almost all other mega-me tropolises like Tokyo, Cairo, Rome, Hong Kong, Bangkok, Bombay, Shanghai, etc. have urban histories dating back thousands of years. Los Angeles is the instant city that grew to 20 million people in one century, perhaps the most rapid growth of any city in history. LA's yearning for the future is mightier than its ties to the past.

There are no age-old traditions to inhibit the growth of the emerging culture. Los Angeles is a restless landscape constantly recreating itself.

Downtown is in the midst of a loft boom. Most of them are adaptive reuse of grand old Banks and such. Numerous loft developments stretch along Spring, Main, 1st, and Broad way to Little Tokyo. Respect to developers like Tom Gilm ore for their vision, but the prices are still too expensive for most artists. Still in less than 5 years a stretch along Main and Spring grew to 22 Galleries. Thanks to Kjell Hagen, Nic, Kimba Rogers & Chayanne this area is now designated by the city *Gallery Row*. Pete's Bar & grill & the Lost Souls Cafe in the alley off 4th Street are crackin'. Museum of Neon Art, Crewest Gallery. Cannibal Flower.

Another new trend is revitalizing old downtown areas in cities like Alhambra, Pomona, Torrance and Whittier. These cities have the traditional main street urban lay out, but they are now being infused with new life. New businesses have plugged into the existing streetscape to make great pedestrian neighborhoods. Urban planners call this "new urbanism." Downtown Alhambra, Pomona and Whittier have vibrant art and music communities with numerous venues.

Chinatown is doing well thanks to the Gold Line and new developments like the art galleries along Chung King Way. But if you ask local Chinese residents about where to get the best Chinese food, they'll tell you to visit the thriving Chinese communities in the San Gabriel Valley of Monterey Park and Alhambra.

The miles and miles of Chinese shops and eateries along streets like Atlantic, Garfield, Garvey and Valley dwarf the original Chinatown. Chinese enclaves now stretches eastward all the way out to Walnut and Diamond Bar.

Similar scenarios correspond to Koreatown, Historic Filipinotown, Thai Town, Little Tokyo and Little Armenia. Suburban cities like Cerritos, Carson, Torrance, Gardena and Glendale have larger populations than the symbolic LA original. After Immigration laws changed in 1965 Asian immigration skyrocketed and districts like Pico-Union swelled with Central Americans escaping civil war.
The flip side of middle class ethnic suburbs is that LA houses more poor immigrants than any other first-world city.
The density in these impoverished districts is comparable to shanty-towns worldwide. Scattered parts of third-world L.A. look like the favelas of Rio De Janeiro in CITY OF GOD. As late as 1960 LA County was one of the Whitest Metroptan areas and one of the leading agricultural counties in the nation.

Will the
boundaries
between different
groups become
faultlines of social conflict
or high voltage generators
of an alternative urban
culture led by
poly-ethnic
vanguards?

Mike Davis
CITY OF QUARTZ,
1990

The answer is both. Yes gang activity is back on the rise, but racism is slowly decreasing with each passing year. Its more about class now. Back in the 50s, 60s, and 70s high schools throughout the Southland had interethnic fighting between White, Black and Brown. There are still some reports like this, but overall tolerance is growing. The younger generations growing up in more diverse neighborhoods are producing more harmony. The widespread prevalence of mixed marriages also tells the story.

Next, the "alternative urban culture" that has been de veloping, especially after 1992 is becoming a force to be reckoned with. A multicultural mix of emerging superstars comprise a new avant-garde unlike anything ever seen. The spirited participants look like the United Nations. A collec tion of amazing characters that transcend race. It's become more about making the art and creating culture. You can feel the scene's magical energy when you visit creative spaces like *Afro Funke, Root Down, Cannibal Flower, Chocolate Bar, A Mic & Dim Lights, 33 1/3rd and Blue Chips.*

In the underground scene, indie is big. Not just indie rock but indie punk hip-hop salsa, you name it. In the days of bling-bling more people than ever are producing intellectu al capital. The rise of the indie scene is a direct response to the difficulties involved in landing a major label record deal or a literary agent. Technology has leveled the playing field and empowered those ready to live their dream.

It only makes sense that Los Angeles is home to thousands of indie artists. Those that stick to their craft eventually find larger audiences. Products of the LA underground like the Beat Junkies, Black Eyed Peas, *Breakestra*, Dilated Peoples, Jurassic 5 and Leonardo DiCaprio all started very humbly.

The common bond of being indie and fighting the good
fight makes the mostly Eastside indie circuit a magical
realm of creativity. Colorful characters like Frohawk Two Feathers
form a mutual admiration society of visual artists, turntablists, pho-
tographers, poets and musicians. As time goes on, genres are melt-
ing. Echo Park indie rockers mix with underground hip-hoppers in
spots like Firecracker in Chinatown. Undercover 'hoods like Elysian
Valley and Atwater Village house Record labels and production com-
panies. Mythical afterhour parties in locations like below the First
Street Bridge have got lots of folks jazzed on
the Eastside scene. Indie labels like *Alpha Pup, Kajmere
Sound, Stones Throw & Up Above* package the under
ground LA sound so the world can hear.
New mayor Antonio Villaraigossa's timing couldn't have
been more perfect. He's a man of the people. His rise
means a lot to the Eastside and epitomizes the underground
hero. Born in the City Terrace part of East LA, he's come
along way to City Hall. LA's newfound maturity provides
the perfect climate to infuse new culture with an exquisite
vitality. LA is now what Athens and Paris were in their
heyday. Much the way Italy was a crossroads for the world
during the Renaissance 500 years ago LA is the crossroads
now. The balance of cultural power has shifted from Eu
rope to the Pacific Rim. Economists have characterized this
shift as the "emerging Asia-oriented economic order."
21st Century Los Angeles represents the newest culmina
tion of global culture. Some have called it "America's cru
cible," or *the postmodern metropolis.* However you slice
it, LA has its own will, its own impetus for change with a
desire to evolve at the same pace as the society that gave it
life. Living in Los Angeles forces one to match the speed
of societal dynamics. As the colliding layers of LA reality
pick up steam it's only going to get more vibrant. It's an
exciting time to be alive in Los Angeles!

Afterhours

The realest hype about Downtown Los Angeles blowing up
has been the consistently jammin' after hour parties over
the last few years. Dating back to the afterhour speakeas
ies of the Prohibition-era, there has always been a magical
mystique about afterhour parties. Take it back to the Har
lem Renaissance. The dance floor seems a little bit darker.
The crowds seem a little bit more wild. Anything goes. It
doesn't hurt that most folks come to the after hours after a
few hours of partying.

Usually held in secretive locations like large brick build
ings in the historic Bank District, rooftops above the Santee
Alley, old warehouses next to the L.A. River, underneath
historic bridges & any other kind of tuckaway you can
imagine like the legendary Chaplin Mansion. Xavier, host
of Club Bingo off deep Main travels the world to say, "L.A.
afterhours are the freshest vibe anywhere." The vibes are
larger than life, extra electric. Most of 'em last until the
sun comes up. Prince showed up on Christmas Eve in the
downtown speakeasy.

The best dj's are all there. The Eastside underground has
so much flavor that it doesn't care who else is there. This
crowd is it. Special multicultural soul style. Magical char
acters like Blackbird, Xavier, Adriana, Longjevity, Han
Cholo, Lisa J, Aceyalone, Kutmah, Emi M., YeM, Karla
Lopez, Felicia, Madlib, Valida, Drrrl, Ronald, Pablo Like
Picasso, Hollywood 7, Josh One, Shakespeare, Mona Lisa,
Liz, Kofie, Jaevi, Rodzilla, Rude One, Lojero, Aztech Sol,
Roz, DoLL One, Dr. Gray, Dusk, Size, Mear One, Mayvon,
Megan J, Miles Tackett, Frohawk, J Logic, Hawkins, ArT,
Coleman, there's so many more of them. Warm energy
glows like an active volcano. The afterhours capture the
zeitgeist of the supreme moment.

The vibe is so incredible that no one ever wants to go home.
The movement!!

7 LA Love & War

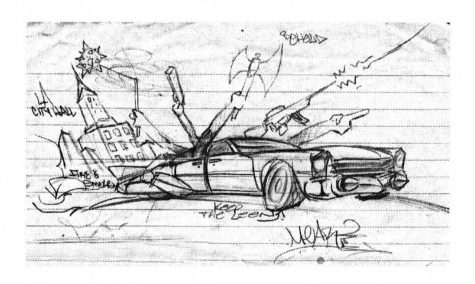

L.A. LOVE & WAR.

People wanna settle
the score
between the haves
& the have nots.
Country clubs
& crooked cops,
Range Rovers
& bus stops.
LA Love & War.
What are we fighting for?

Inner-city Salvadorans have seen civil war,
Like in Israel, Resentment is real,
everybody wants a better deal.
Shotgun blasts & the battle for ca$h—
Have you seen *The Fast & the Furious*?
Interracial lovers & racist gangsters
Crystallize vibes on street corners
Making love & making war.
Check the Mythical folklore
the news talks about race wars in Compton
Zoot Suit riots, Watts & Rodney King.
Santa Ana winds & earthquakes,
in every way the city shakes.
Life in the Golden State got people on the make,
Class lines define public space making
a geography of rage in a built environment
Built For retirement. Anglo geriatrics & job dispersion
Economic shifts & immigration.
Unemployment & inflation, ecstasy & frustration,
AfroAsianLatinization, Art kids & bohemians,

The fusion of multicultural unions
produces beautiful children.
Neighborhoods blend
like a DJ mixing records,

West Adams Country Club Park Koreatown
the Rampart, East Hollywood Echo Park
gang sweeps & North Long Beach,
beats match As buildings blend socioeconomics.
Mansions housing projects skyscraper crack houses.
The citizens mix like *jambalaya*—
LA Love & War.

Its no coincidence City hall
is shaped like a phallic symbol,
Parking tickets & taxes sodomize citizens with no
Lubrication & its mostly the poor ones.
Immigrants come to California
looking for gold but end up on Western.
Everybody wants the American dream.
Come Get your ca$h cream.
Rampart cops selling drugs for profit
Sleeping with hookers on the clock.
This is where the angels got lost
& they wonder why everybody's so pissed off.
LA Love & War.

Rainbow coalitions become broken rainbows
Snipers on rooftops, ghetto birds on the simulcast,
News flash!
Don't slip on the broken glass,
citizens are on the attack taking the city back.
A soundtrack of gangsta rap, Simon says get the buck up.
Kinko's is across from Starbucks,
Ice Cube to Mitchell Crooks,
Reginald Denny to Tupac.
A bottle of juice is no excuse,
The truth hurts.
Korean liquor stores,
crack whores,
drug wars.

Interracial lovers & racist gangsters
Crystallize vibes on street corners
The fluorescent fires burn bright flames,
Making babies & making graves.
Flames from the '92 Riots were so bright
They could be seen from space,
That's how hot it gets in this place.
LA Love & war.
Aware citizens need tolerance & compassion,
Recognize your blessings & stop fighting.
All this brewing energy
should be used for building.
broken rainbows can become bridges,
If your alive in Los Angeles,
organize your ish as rightly burning!

We are the difference
and the world is turning.

LA Love & War,

People wanna settle the score
between the haves & the have nots
Country clubs & crooked cops,
Range Rovers & bus stops.
LA Love & War.

*WE DON'T NEED TO FIGHT
NO MORE!*

Frequently Asked Questions.

There is no question that Los Angeles is a fragmented metropolis. Many urban theorists have used terms like "spatial apartheid," and "Balkanization," to characterize the sometimes explosive race relations and segregated neigh borhoods of the Southland. Longtime Angelinos know that there is definitely a split between East & West Los Angeles. What about South Central, the Valley, Long Beach, Orange County & the Inland Empire? Here's a breakdown for the record.

Where exactly is the Eastside & What is the physical boundary?

OG eastsiders like Ulises Diaz & Luis Rodriguez tell me east of the Los Angeles River is the start of East LA. Others have said that it starts 2 miles west of the river, east of the 110 freeway. Many have called Silverlake, Echo Park & even East Hollywood part of the Eastside. Some people even say La Brea is the start of the Eastside. There has been talk of the Eastside indie rock circuit of Silverlake & Echo Park. The answer just depends on who it is, where they live & where they wanna be down from.

Where is the Westside?

The Westside of Los Angeles really begins just west of La Cienega moving towards Robertson. Beverly Hills west is usually considered the start of the westside. West LA, Santa Monica, Brentwood, Westwood, Venice, Pacific Palisades & beyond. 310 all the way to the South Bay.

Where is South Central?

South Central means to many Angeli nos south of the 10 Freeway. It's a common

assumption that overlooks specific neighborhood history. The wide area south of the 10 lumped in as South Central is a giant pocket of land well over 40 square miles. Arteries like Crenshaw, Avalon, Adams, Jefferson, Slauson, Florence, Manchester. It's a construct that has been mythologized. It's a huge part of southern Los Angeles comprised of small districts like Angeles Mesa, Canterbury Knolls, Jefferson Park, Green Meadows, Chesterfield Square, Manchester Square & more.

The roots of Los Angeles African-American Community is histori-cally thought of as Watts, down around Central Avenue, 103rd & Willowbrook. Watts is about 7 miles south east of USC & the 110-10 Freeway. Nonetheless, over the last 30 years or so *Leimert Park* around Crenshaw & 43rd has emerged as the center of the Black community.

Where is Orange County?
Ironically Orange County is statistically more urban than Los Angeles County. The explanation is that the whole
northern third of LA County is desert & mountain land, while damn near every square foot of land in Orange
County is packed with development. The OC is one of the most urban counties in America. In 2006 after the recent FOX TV show *The OC* & M-TV's *Laguna Beach,* the OC proclaims itself as the "mecca" of cool. Some used to call it the *Orange Curtain.* It just depends where you're from & what you believe in.

Census figures over the last 20 years show local areas like Long Beach, Gardena & Carson are as diverse as any place in North America. Here is where you see the future of America. Among the generation growing up in this melting pot is a compassionate group of people concerned with keeping peace & building a better future.

Some have called it utopian, our hopes lie in working together. Building community is where it's at. Pockets of community are villages in the sprawling mosaic. Bridge builders are wiring a circuitry of unity through the patchwork. For those willing to reach out of their comfort zone, the possibilities are endless & never boring.

SPANGLISH IS OUR SECOND LANGUAGE

One of the largest gatherings in downtown history culminated with protestors blocking the 101& 110 Freeways draped in Mexican flags. Davey D wrote, "Trust me more than a million people
showed up. Anyone who was there could attest to that. All the blocks around the courthouse for as far as the eye could see was a sea of people. It was wall to wall."
Surprise! California has become what it already was, Latin. Demographic changes have happened so fast over the last 40 years that Latinos are now the majority in the City of
Angels. Asian immigration has skyrocketed since 1965. Los Angeles was once one of the most lily-white metropolises. In the 21st Century it is the epitome of cultural diversity.
Some people build walls, others build bridges.

One result is *Spanglish*, a hybrid, universal language, the fusing of English & Spanish. It's a colloquial language that utilizes a little bit of sign language & repeated key phrases. It often takes compassion & patience to engage in the dialogue. Examples of Spanglish are all over our street signs like your local *Mexicatessan*. This isn't just Los Angeles. It's Miami, San Antonio, New York City, San Diego, To ronto, London & so on.
California is occupied Mexico.
New York, Puerto Rico.
Dominican, cinnamon
Spanish speaking Nuyorican.
Salvadoran Salvatrucha
Pacoima to Pomona,
there's nothing like a torta
from your local roach coach.
I get mine @ 8th Street in Koreatown
Spanglish is our second language.

Universal worldwide tribe people
know we live in a super diverse world,
why not a universal language?

Spanish English
Japanese Korean
Armenian, everything.
Life in the urban melting pot
got a lot of flavor.

Celebrate the mosaic,
make language fun,
creativity comes from
the context of each situation.

Semiotics is communication,
the next level of interaction
is an accelerated pidgin,
a pure product of evolution.
The process happens over generations,
in California there's a new nation
combining the best of all languages.
One global human family.

We can all get along!

LiVIN' THE DREAM.

To dream is

to aspire

for something
great;

a fanciful vision,

an aspiration.

California has

always

been a place

for dreamers.

Dreams of gold brought 49ers to California.
200 years before gold brought the Conquistadors!

They're still coming to get more, Come & get yours!
Score! More, more, more!

California!
Dreamers have been coming for centuries.
Sailing the Cape Horn, moving on the stage coach,
the transcontinental railroad,
Coming to California to get gold!

Prospectors on a quest
in the wild, wild west, the sky's the limit!

California dreamin'.

Immigrants, transplants,
old Spanish land grants,
Some come for love, some come for promotions,
step into a sea of emotions,
some people come here & lose their minds.
Everything is within an arm's reach,
but most can't reach.
Greedy developers stole water from the *Owens Valley.*
Okies built squatter camps one room at a time,
backyard-chicken-coop-hen-houses precluded trailer parks.

It's hard to believe open space once defined this place.
Restrictive HOUSING COVENANTS
kept Blacks west of Alameda.
Rosie the Riveter was in the factory

At the same time
Japanese families were uprooted
& sent to Internment Camps, they lost *everything*.
The dream is victory, defeat, ecstasy, agony,
Gambling on the California dream.!

Boosters, bangers,
Baptists, bachelors,
actors, beautiful actresses,
fire starters burn yours in Los Angeles!
We livin' the dream in an archipelago
of swimming pools, garage sales, county jails,
million dollar homes, mini malls, swap meets.
The picket fence & Gidget
have given way to ridiculous rent,
gridlock, homeless & gangsters.

The dream has been manufactured,
while the manufacturing jobs moved over seas.
The dream is locked up in gated communities.
Golf courses lie next to Joshua trees
and Indian casinos blast high powered air conditioning.
Salvadoran sidewalk vendors
sell bacon-wrapped sausages,
neon lights up high-rise offices.
Soccer moms in the San Fernando Valley
sip lattes in SUV's;
cookie cutter architecture characterizes the OC,
O.J. Simpson scored touchdowns at USC;
you know he was livin' the dream!

& even Reginald Denny has a star on the Hollywood
Walk of Fame.
Earthquakes, labor strikes, mudslides,
riots, forest fires, nuclear skies,
the dream never dies!
Bonzo Ronald Reagan, Raving,
two-way paging, escapism, public problems,
private schools. Dreams won & dreams lost!
Real estate costs, Biggie got shot,
Blood, sweat & tears
it's Explosive! Open, broken, hoping
buildings smoking, Sunset to Slauson,
Pomona to Compton. Burnt down back draft.
Paranoid backlash! Xenophobic racists
move to Arizona, they can't handle *Mexifornia,*
white flight out to Idaho.
I'm here to let you know,
that all those who have left,
stepped, crept out of California,
we won't miss you 'cuz 5 more
just like you crossed the border.
Operation Gatekeeper forces
would-be migrants to cut across
sand dunes in triple digit temperatures,
over 2,000 have died trying
since the mid '90's; they keep coming.

Property prices keep climbin' higher,
some move out to the Inland Empire,
longtime commuters become war veterans
to reconcile paychecks with mortgages.
If you want higher wages move to Las Vegas.

Franchises that once flourished
are now gone like they were never there.
Perino's, Ships, Ambassador—
(Wasn't there a street called *Cinnabar?*)
Single mothers work double shifts to keep the family fed.
Hells Angels on Harley hogs ride into the wind,
California dreamin'.
Take a ride on The Pacific Coast Highway,
see the flashes over Disneyland.

Fires burn in the chaparral as what was once heaven becomes hell,
but what some consider hell is heaven to those who have come from
somewhere else.

The golden dream on the coast.
Come & get yours! California!

Get your rolling blackouts, aspiring starlets, white trash chic, 818
pornography, Vin Scully, Kareem, Chick Hearn, Fernando
Valenzuela, Magic Johnson, the Hollywood Canteen, *Chavez Ravine.*

Dream! Dream! Dream!
Law & order in California equals fame & fortune, Michael
Jackson, Kobe Bryant, Phil Specter. Arnold Schwarzenegger!
The terminator, the governator, the *gropenator,* alien alienator,
carboquaker, steroid taker, firefight faker.
He better be a job maker!
Let's get this party pumping Arnold!

One time
for your mind Los Angeles!

Fiesta forever, Cali lovers of culture congregate in the golden state for a soul shake down, buoyant sounds are building the wave for a brand new day & we'll be dancin' the way the Californios did when California belonged to Mexico, everything old is new again.

Gabrielino Indians know the Village by the River has always been Mexican.

One day the Concrete River will be unpaved, a free flowing flood-plain flowing the way it did when La Brea was tar pits. Check this New Age renaissance, the rebirth of Hollywood, *Dogtown & Z-Boys,*

The SOUL FORCE FOR PEACE
is surfing waves in California,

LIVIN' THE DREAM!

An ode to my city!

Neon crowns
glow above
The City of Angels.
Haze hovers after
another nuclear sunset,
I love it all.
I am alive in
Los Angeles!

ACKNOWLEDGEMENTS

God, Mom, Mear One, P.M., Dad,
Emi M, Lee Ballinger, Mike Davis,
Amy, Frank & Shirley

Extra large respect to the Poets of the Round Table. Thank you!
PhiLLHarmoniC, DJ DAVE, Besskepp, Stricke9, Ordell Cordova,
Tone Tec, 7, Blackbird, J Sole, Sarah Cruse, Megan Jacobs, Dr. Gray,
Yem, Bintu, Mear One, Ratpack Slim, Sean Morris.

BooyakashaW! Blessings out to Jointz Magazine, Kotori,
Kajmere SOUND, Henry, Tyler, Jasper, EARL, Kwon, DJ
Dave, Yem, Raymond@LOST, Karl, Devin, Blaine, Khalid
& Motion, the Blue Nile Café, Russ, Vic & all my friends
on Normandale Ave, Rude One, Blue Chips, Herbie, Karla,
Davey D, Museum of Neon Art, Straight No Chaser, Wilshire
Words, URB, Luis Rodriguez, Fidel Rodriguez, Lewis
MacAdams, Divine Forces Radio, Word Space, Poetroni
girL, Brenda Varda, Rebirth, Breakestra, Loslito, Llaves,
the Goat, Aztech Sol, Wanda Coleman, Jennifer Cuevas,
Jon Ship, IMIX Books, UP Above, LMNO, Key Kool,
LD & Ariano, Skylight Books, James Dunn, Saul Wil
liams, Cary, Rocky, Crown City Rockers, Raashan, Cole
man, Hawkins, Dusk, DJ Haul & Mason, Wyatt Case, TIA
Chuchas, the Giant Peach, Beyond Baroque, Temple Bar,
Anthony Valadez, Southern California Research Library,
Carolyn See, Kevin Starr, Open, UCLA, KPFK, B+, LA
WEEKLY, OC Weekly, LA Record, LA Alternative Press,
P.C., Technicali, Cizmar, Jeff Smith, Dave & Mary Elaine
Sonksen. Livingroom Johnston & you!
God BleSS!

MIKE THE POET

Mike Sonksen, also known as, "Mike the Poet," is a 3rd generation L.A. native. Whether you see his work on the page or the stage it radiates life. Mike is a writer on a mission. As a Poet Journalist Spoken Word Artist he's widely acclaimed for his live performances and frequent contributions to national publications. For over a decade, Mike's performed at numerous venues: bookstores, museums, nightclubs, art galleries, churches, you name it. Published in the *Los Angeles Times, Anthem, KOTORI, L.A. Weekly, L.A. Citybeat, L.A Record, L.A. Alternative Press, O.C. Weekly, Long Beach Business Journal*, etc. Mike is Music Editor for the monthly, Jointz Mag and co-founder of the webzine Getunderground.com. He hosts monthly gigs @ the Blue Nile Cafe & Blue Chips. Mike performed his poem "LA. Authors," @ the L.A. Times Book Prizes. His poem *The Best Minds of My Generation*, was licensed by Scion to appear on the mix CD: "Labeless Lifestyles."
Mike's been featured on Eye on LA, KKBT, Divine Forces Radio, Music Plus TV. Mike has also been a tourguide for several companies including Red Line Tours & his poetic tours around Los Angeles sponsored by the Museum of Neon Art. Mike graduated from UCLA in 1997.

Holla @ him 'cuz he likes people.
mikethepoet@comcast.net
www.myspace.com/mikethepoet

Cover & illustrations by MEAR ONE
MEAR ONE is an L.A. legend. His work can be found in major art galleries, 40+ album covers & magazines. Check his website for more.
www.mearone.com

TRACK ORDER OF
I AM ALIVE IN LOS ANGELES!
C.D.

I AM ALIVE IN LOS ANGELES!
THE EMPEROR WEARS NO CLOTHES
CENTRAL CALI'S COAST CRESCENDO
HOLLYWOOD
THE BEST MINDS OF MY GENERATION
L.A. AUTHORS
POP
DENSITY
RHAPSODY
NOW I'M OLDER (D.J. DAVE)
L.A. LOVE & WAR
DANCIN' TIMES

Produced by D.J. DAVE
www.ksdmusic.com
REVIEWS...

"The appeal of I Am Alive in Los Angeles is its effortlessness. It's political without telling you to wear a badge or jump on any bandwagon and its funny wihout the neon-colored punchlines. All lovers of intricate wordplay, add this to your list."—Straight No Chaser

"Mike The Poet sings the flatlands and the mean streets. In the City of Quartz, he is his generation's Walt Whitman."—Mike Davis

"Mike the PoeT is at the vanguard of a burgeoning. multicultural spoken word/art/hip-hop movement."
BLISS—Pasadena Weekly

"The most prolific spoken word poet in Los Angeles County—an Angelino poet to the bone—Sonksen understands the Southland megalopolis as well as anyone, but it's his ability to fuse modern urban images with timeless raconteur themes that will ensure his work stands the test of time."-Tyler Reeb, Editor of The Southlander & the Long Beach Business Journal

"This cat has the ability to not only speak as a poet's poet-
in metaphors, cadence, and description-but also articulate
the smells, touch, and taste of the world around him in such
a fundamental manner you leave the listening session ex
cited about re-touching life. Get re-inspired about existence
in L.A.! Viva Mike the Poet!"—Raashan Ahmad (Crown
City Rockers)
"I Am Alive In Los Angeles is the perfect title for this collage of lush production and the slick stylings of Mike The Poet. His approach to each track is in the purest form of futuristic poetry…"-DJ Josh One

"Working over tracks that are a little bit hip-hop and a
whole lot of drum 'n bass, Mike Sonksen speaks for the
new breed he's part of on "The Best Minds of My Generation" only
to turn around and give props to all who came before on "L.A.
Authors." He glories in the melting pot
that is today's Los Angeles with a spy satellite's eye for
detail, yet doesn't shy away from describing all who get
boiled to death on that stove. The masterpiece is "L.A.
Love and War," which begins: "L.A. love and war/People want to set-
tle the score/Between the haves and the have
nots/Country clubs and the crooked cops/Range Rovers and the bus
stops/L.A. love and war/What are we fighting for?" Sonksen answers
that question with a fierce poetic fury,
presenting a jaw-dropping panorama that just keeps rolling, rolling,
rolling like a river."—(Rock & Rap Confidential)

"After being on the Westside for more than one hour, I
always need to decompress with an Eastside event, usually Mike the
Poet is good for providing this kind of envi
ronment, if I were given the power to sanction the most bad-ass
reading of the month I would have to give it to
Mike the Poet & the Poets of the Roundtable, he runs Blue Chips, he
runs 33 1/3, and now he runs a reading at Zen Sushi, Outside the
Box, every second Wednesday, spoken word artists, literary artists,
visual artists, musical art
ists; artists, artists, everywhere, it's awesome, the best run eclectic
reading in poetry, Mike's venues are always worth it. Mike the Poet
the most cool, positive guy in poetry, future LA legend you read it
here first."—TEKA LARK LO
Rest in Power DJ DusK. The man born as Tarek Captan was a music-
man, teacher & great friend of Los Angeles. His light burned bright
in his quick action packed life. DJ DusK lived his devotion for the
city of Angels. "And I say One time for your mind Los Angeles! If
you're feelin alright now, make some motherfu#$in nooooiise!!"
Thanks Dusk.. You were truly ahead of time. We're not done.

978-0-595-39520-0
0-595-39520-1

Printed in the United States
53576LVS00005B/250-348